the
mother
of all
pregnancy
organizers

ANN DOUGLAS

Copyright © 2004 Wiley, Hoboken, NJ
Published by Wiley, Hoboken, NJ
Published simultaneously in Canada

Library of Congress Control Number: 2004101607
ISBN: 0-7645-5913-3

Manufactured in **China**
10 9 8 7 6 5 4 3 2
Book design by **Kathie S. Schnorr**
Cover design by **Wendy Mount**
Page creation by Wiley Publishing, Inc. Composition Services

Praise for *The Mother of All Pregnancy Organizers*

Every pregnancy is unique, but expectant moms all have one thing in common: They have a million different things on their minds and another thousand on their to-do lists. Ann Douglas's *The Mother Of All Pregnancy Organizers* is the perfect tool to help keep you sane, let you stay ahead of the curve, and get you prepared for your new baby. Keep track of shopping trips, pick up helpful tips on everything from morning sickness to recognizing signs of labor — and even record your own little notes to help you remember all those little details you never, ever want to forget.

— *Nancy Price, Editor/Founder,* PregnancyAndBaby.com *and* ShowingMagazine.com

Ann Douglas is an organizational wonder. Whether you're interested in keeping track of your prenatal visits, figuring out what baby essentials to stock up on, remembering what to take to the hospital, or just learning how the heck to manage pregnancy and impending motherhood, Douglas's amazingly comprehensive book will make life easier for anyone who is on the journey toward becoming a mother.

— *Andrea J. Buchanan, author,* Mother Shock: Loving Every (Other) Minute of It

Dr. Spock may have steadied our foothold on parenting with purpose, but Ann Douglas, the great guru of all things pregnancy, leaves no stone unturned when it comes to pregnancy, labor, and birth. Informative and honest, Douglas crafts a must-read for pregnant women and their partners. She understands both the miracle and the mystery of birth and offers practical, no-nonsense advice for every situation. If you're pregnant or considering pregnancy, she should be your go-to-gal — before your first check-up!

— *Julia Rosien, Senior Editor,* News and Notes, ePregnancy:
Your Everything Pregnancy Magazine!

How to Use the Organizer

This organizer is designed to help you keep track of all the exciting details that go into planning for a healthy pregnancy and getting ready for life in your post-baby universe. In the six sections of this organizer, you not only have a place to jot down information that's genuinely useful to you and your doctor or midwife, you also have a once-in-a-lifetime opportunity to create a very special memento of your pregnancy and the early weeks with your new baby.

Section I — Operation Healthy Baby

In this section of the organizer, you can record your earliest signs of pregnancy, note the types of questions you would like to ask when you're interviewing potential doctors or midwives, and log details about your prenatal visits and any medications you're taking.

Section II — Your Weekly Planner

This section provides you with a weekly journal in which you can record the physical and emotional changes that you experience over the course of your pregnancy. You can also use these pages to note your most memorable moments, from your baby's first flutters and kicks to the happy reactions of friends and family to the results of ultrasounds. We're talking the stuff of which memories are made!

Section III — Revving Up For Baby

This section of the organizer helps you gather up all the supplies you need to have on hand after you deliver your baby — everything from buying a car seat to hardware that makes your baby's room safe. You can keep track of any stores where you and your baby are registered; you're also reminded of who gave you those lovely baby shower gifts. And when it comes time to start interviewing potential pediatricians, this section will prove to be a real lifesaver, offering both a checklist of questions to ask and spaces for the prospective pediatrician's responses.

Section IV — Gearing Up for Delivery

In this next section of the planner, you find tips and advice for the last few weeks before you're due. (Yep, things are getting serious by the time you get this far into the organizer.) You can keep track of details about your prenatal and breastfeeding classes and any scheduled hospital tours so that you don't miss out on anything. You also get the lowdown on putting your post-baby support team in place, from finding out who can drive you to the hospital to knowing who can help you cook meals during that first crazy week at home. You keep track of what final arrangements you need to make, get an inventory of what to pack in your bags, and fill in lists of people to call after your baby is born. (Hey, they don't call this an organizer for nothing!)

Section V — Baby's Grand Entrance

Not sure whether it's labor or a false alarm? This section helps you to figure out whether your baby is about to make his or her grand entrance. After your baby is born, you can track test results and pediatrician visits and jot down advice from your caregivers on everything from bathing your baby to breastfeeding to caring for your own postpartum body. You'll find a birth-announcement organizer and places to note the gifts your baby receives after the birth. (You won't believe how many gifts your baby will receive.) Finally, you have the chance to jot down all the questions you have for your doctor or midwife at your follow-up visit.

Section VI — Resource Guide

This section is a quick resource guide that offers tips and advice on which foods to avoid and which to indulge in, what medications to steer clear of, and when you should get in touch with your doctor or midwife right away to seek emergency medical care. You also learn about the symptoms of premature labor and postpartum depression — essential info for any mom-to-be. Finally, you get a set of blank calendar pages. Use them to keep track of all of your appointments (pregnancy related or not) in one place so that you don't miss a beat over the next ten crazy months of your life.

Operation Healthy Baby

The moment the sperm and the egg hooked up in the darkest recesses of your fallopian tube, you signed on for a super-secret mission called Operation Healthy Baby — a mission so secret, in fact, that for the first few weeks of your pregnancy, you didn't even know you'd been recruited!

Super-secret spy stuff aside, your mission over the next nine months is pretty straightforward: to do everything in your power to maximize your chances of having a healthy baby. That means gaining a healthy amount of weight, ensuring that your body gets an ample supply of nutrients, and avoiding substances that could be harmful to your baby.

This section helps you keep track of both your health and the health of your growing fetus throughout your pregnancy. In between discovering useful tips on choosing a caregiver and detailed information about what to expect in your prenatal visits, you'll also find pages to record your first signs of pregnancy, write down the addresses and phone numbers of your caregivers, fill in information that your caregiver will ask for at your first visit, and keep an eye on any medications you're taking.

This section also helps you log your first and 14 subsequent prenatal visits to your caregiver. These pages provide spaces for the time and date of each visit with your caregiver — fill these in as you schedule each appointment, and you'll never miss a prenatal visit! You'll also find areas to note the multitude of questions you have for your doctor or midwife, as well as space to jot down his or her recommendations. For each prenatal visit, you'll also find a reassuring tip or fact that may help to eliminate at least one of your worries, as well as room to write down your current health statistics, such your estimated due date, weight, blood pressure, pulse, test results, and contractions. Throughout your pregnancy, you can also use this section to keep track of your baby's health information, including his or her fetal heart rate and fundal height (the distance from the top of your pubic bone to the top of your uterus; a way of measuring your baby's growth).

First Signs of Pregnancy

Are you experiencing the first signs of pregnancy or is something else going on? This table identifies common symptoms and also highlights other causes of those symptoms.

Symptom	What Causes It to Occur During Pregnancy	Other Possible Causes
Menstrual Changes		
A missed period	Rising levels of progesterone fully suppress your menstrual period.	Birth control pills, jet lag, extreme weight loss or gain, a change in climate, a chronic disease such as diabetes or tuberculosis, severe illness, surgery, shock, bereavement, or other sources of stress.
A lighter-than-average period	Your progesterone levels are rising, but not enough to fully suppress your menstrual period (making your due date difficult to pinpoint).	Can be experienced by users of birth control pills.
A small amount of spotting	May occur when the fertilized egg implants in the uterine wall — about a week after conception has occurred.	Can be experienced by users of birth control pills and women with fibroids or infections. What's more, some women routinely experience some mid-cycle spotting. Spotting may also be the earliest sign of an impending miscarriage.

Symptom	What Causes It to Occur During Pregnancy	Other Possible Causes
Breast Changes		
Breast tenderness and enlargement	Hormonal changes of early pregnancy. Note: You may also notice some related physical changes. The areola (the flat area around the nipple) may begin to darken, and the tiny glands on the areola may begin to enlarge.	Premenstrual syndrome (PMS), excessive caffeine intake, or fibrocystic breast disease.
Cramping and/or Nausea		
Abdominal cramping (period-like cramping in the lower abdomen and pelvis and/or bloating and gassiness)	Hormonal changes of early pregnancy.	PMS, constipation, or irritable bowel syndrome.
Morning sickness (used to describe everything from mild nausea to vomiting to the point of dehydration)	High levels of progesterone and human chorionic gonadotropin (hCG). Note: Tends to be worse first thing in the morning, when your blood sugar is at its lowest.	Flu, food poisoning, or other illnesses.
Increased Need to Urinate and/or Constipation		
Increased need to urinate	Increased blood flow to the pelvic area, triggered by the production of human chorionic gonadotropin (hCG) during early pregnancy.	A urinary tract infection, uterine fibroids, or excessive caffeine intake.
Constipation	Progesterone relaxes the intestinal muscles, resulting in varying degrees of constipation.	Inadequate intake of high-fiber foods or inadequate consumption of fluids.

Symptom	What Causes It to Occur During Pregnancy	Other Possible Causes
Food Aversions and Cravings and/or Heightened Sense of Smell		
Food aversions and cravings (e.g., a metallic taste in the mouth and/or a craving for certain foods)	Hormonal changes of early pregnancy.	Poor diet, stress, or PMS.
Heightened sense of smell	Hormonal changes of early pregnancy.	Illness.
Decreased Energy Level		
Fatigue	Increased production of progesterone (which acts as a natural sedative) and an increase in your metabolic rate (your body's way of ensuring it will be able to support the needs of you and your developing baby).	Not getting enough sleep, not eating properly, flu, illness, or some other medical condition.
Changes to the Reproductive Organs		
Changes to the cervix (slightly purplish hue; softening) and the uterus (softening)	Hormonal changes of early pregnancy (detected by your doctor or midwife during a pelvic examination).	A delayed menstrual period.

The Moment You Knew

Record details of when you first knew you were pregnant:

_____

_____

_____

_____

_____

Mini Address Book

Keep track of caregivers who can help you through both pregnancy and the early months of your baby's life: your primary care physician, OB/GYN, nurse-midwife, doula (a professional labor support person), childbirth educator, lactation consultant, and more.

Name of caregiver: _____
Role: _____
Affiliation: _____
Address: _____
Phone number: _____
E-mail address and/or Web site: _____

Name of caregiver: _____
Role: _____
Affiliation: _____
Address: _____
Phone number: _____
E-mail address and/or Web site: _____

Name of caregiver: _____
Role: _____
Affiliation: _____
Address: _____
Phone number: _____
E-mail address and/or Web site: _____

Name of caregiver: _____
Role: _____
Affiliation: _____
Address: _____
Phone number: _____
E-mail address and/or Web site: _____

Mini Address Book

Name of caregiver: _____
Role: _____
Affiliation: _____
Address: _____
Phone number: _____
E-mail address and/or Web site: _____

Name of caregiver: _____
Role: _____
Affiliation: _____
Address: _____
Phone number: _____
E-mail address and/or Web site: _____

Name of caregiver: _____
Role: _____
Affiliation: _____
Address: _____
Phone number: _____
E-mail address and/or Web site: _____

Name of caregiver: _____
Role: _____
Affiliation: _____
Address: _____
Phone number: _____
E-mail address and/or Web site: _____

Name of caregiver: _____
Role: _____
Affiliation: _____
Address: _____
Phone number: _____
E-mail address and/or Web site: _____

Choosing Your Caregiver

At this stage of the game, you're probably worried about finding a doctor or midwife to care for you during your pregnancy and to be present at the birth of your baby. Here are some specific questions to ask when you're trying to determine whether a particular caregiver is right for you:

How long have you been in practice? _____

How many births have you attended? _____

What percentage of your patients' babies do you end up delivering yourself? _____

What's your standard schedule for prenatal appointments? _____

Under what circumstances would you decide to see me more often than this? _____

How much time do you set aside for each appointment? _____

What types of tests are you likely to recommend over the course of my pregnancy (e.g., ultrasound, maternal-serum screening, amniocentesis, gestational diabetes, group B strep)? _____

Under what circumstances, if any, would you need to transfer me into the care of another health-care provider and/or specialist? _____

Other than you, who might be present at the birth of my baby? _____

Do you involve residents, interns, or student midwives in your practice? If so, what role would they play in my care? _____

How often are you on call? _____

Do you expect to be on call around the time that my baby is due? _____

How should I go about reaching you in the event of an emergency? _____

What hospitals and/or birth centers are you affiliated with? _____

Choosing Your Caregiver

Do you attend home births? _____

How much time will you be able to spend with me while I'm in labor?

_____

Under what circumstances do you induce labor? _____

_____

Do the majority of women who you care for have medicated or non-medicated births? _____

When medicated, which methods of pharmacological and non-pharmacological pain relief do they tend to use the most often (e.g., epidurals vs. laboring in water)? _____

_____

Do you encourage couples to attempt unmedicated deliveries? _____

How would you feel if I were to decide to use the services of a doula or some other labor support person? _____

Do you routinely use electronic fetal monitoring during labor? _____

What percentage of women in your care receive episiotomies? _____

How often do the women in your care end up delivering through cesarean section? _____

What percentage of the women in your care who are attempting a vaginal birth after cesarean (VBAC) are able to deliver vaginally? _____

_____

Will my baby be able to remain with me after the birth? _____

_____

Do you provide breastfeeding support? _____

How often will I see you during the postpartum period? _____

_____

Should my baby be checked by another health-care provider during this period? _____

Preparing for Your First Prenatal Visit

Regardless of whether you intend to give birth at home or in the hospital, and to be cared for by a midwife, family physician, or obstetrician, you'll want to get in to see your caregiver as soon as possible after you find out that you're pregnant. This is particularly important if your pregnancy was unplanned and you weren't able to schedule a preconception checkup. Before heading to your first prenatal visit, use this checklist to assemble information that your doctor or midwife needs to know about you.

❑ Date of first day of your most recent period: _____

❑ What types of vitamins you take (if any) and if you are likely to have any nutritional deficiencies or other dietary concerns that could have an impact on your pregnancy. Details about these concerns are:
_____

❑ Lifestyle information, including whether and how much you exercise, whether you smoke, how much (if any) alcohol you consume each week, and whether you are exposed to any hazardous materials or working conditions on the job

❑ Your obstetrical and gynecological history, including prior pregnancies or miscarriages, tests and surgeries, and any gynecological problems

❑ Your general medical history (not necessarily related to child-bearing), including chronic medical problems, surgeries, and allergies

❑ Medications you're taking: _____

❑ Your immunizations, including those you had as a child (Note: You may want to consult with an older family member if you're not sure about your childhood immunization history.)

❑ Any fertility charts you and your partner have been keeping while trying to conceive

❑ Make sure your caregiver will have access to any results of blood or urine tests you've had over the last ten years, including tests for diabetes or hypoglycemia, cholesterol screenings, hepatitis tests, HIV tests, and so on. (Note: This may require a phone call or a fax on your part.)

Preparing for Your First Prenatal Visit

Your prenatal visit will also focus on your and your partner's medical history, and it will probably also include the medical history of your baby's grandparents, aunts, and uncles.

	You	Your Husband/ Partner	Your Siblings	Your Partner's Siblings	Your Mother	Your Father	Your Partner's Mother	Your Partner's Father	Other Relatives
Cerebral palsy									
Cystic fibrosis									
Hemophilia									
Mental retardation									
Muscular dystrophy									
Neural tube defects, including spina bifida									
Sickle-cell anemia									
Tay-Sachs									
Thalassemia									
*Other genetic diseases									

*Other genetic diseases:

Your First Prenatal Visit

During your initial prenatal checkup, your caregiver may do some or all of the following:

- Confirm your pregnancy by doing a urine or blood test or by conducting a physical examination

- Estimate your due date by considering a range of factors

- Perform a blood test to check for illnesses and, if necessary, certain genetic diseases

- Take a vaginal culture to check for infection

- Do a Pap smear to check for cervical cancer or pre-cancerous cells

- Check your urine for signs of infection, blood sugar problems, and excess protein

- Weigh you to establish a baseline so that your weight gain during pregnancy can be monitored

- Take your blood pressure

Your practitioner is also likely to want to discuss:

- Whether you'll be working during your pregnancy (and, if so, whether you'll require any work modifications for safety reasons)

- Whether there are any special circumstances that he/she should know about in order to care for you during your pregnancy and birth (e.g., whether you have a history of sexual abuse that might lead to heightened anxiety about the birth; whether there are any ethnic or religious traditions that might affect your pregnancy and your child's birth)

- Whether you have any questions or concerns

Your First Prenatal Visit

Records and Other Notes

Your doctor or midwife will record details about your pregnancy on your prenatal record. He or she may also provide you with a patient version of this record so that you can keep your own pregnancy records, as well. Jot down your results here so you will have your baseline medical statistics handy to compare when necessary at subsequent checkups.

Your estimated due date: _____

Your weight: _____

Your blood pressure: _____

Your pulse: _____

Results of our urine test: _____

_____

_____

_____

Results of any blood test(s): _____

_____

_____

_____

Results of your vaginal culture: _____

_____

_____

Results of your Pap smear: _____

_____

_____

Results of any other tests and exams: _____

_____

_____

Your First Prenatal Visit

Q&A

Got a million questions? That's to be expected at this stage of the game. Be sure to ask your doctor or midwife whatever's on your mind, even if it feels like a game of Twenty Questions. Use this page to list questions you and your partner want to ask, so that you don't miss a single one.

Your First Prenatal Visit

Going Forward

You're likely to talk to your doctor or midwife about all kinds of things during your first prenatal visit — so much, in fact, that it can be difficult to remember everything that was discussed. You may want to make a few notes during your appointment so that you can refer back to these notes during the weeks ahead.

Prenatal Visit 2

Q&A

Questions to ask your doctor or midwife:

_____

_____

_____

_____

_____

_____

_____

_____

_____

_____

_____

_____

_____

_____

_____

_____

_____

 At eight weeks, your baby's teeth, palate, and larynx are beginning to take shape. The baby is now approximately 1¼ inches long — the size of a large grape. At nine weeks, the baby's organs, muscles, and nerves begin to function, and it begins to make its first spontaneous movements — movements that are far too tiny for you to detect at this stage of your pregnancy.

Prenatal Visit 2

Stats and Test Results

Use this page to record the stats and test results from this prenatal visit.

Date and time of visit: _____

Weight: _____

Blood pressure: _____

Pulse: _____

Urinalysis results: _____

Fetal heart rate: _____

Fundal height: _____

Other test results: _____

Going Forward

Recommendations and advice from your caregiver:

_____

_____

_____

_____

_____

_____

_____

_____

_____

_____

_____

Prenatal Visit 3

Q&A

Questions to ask your doctor or midwife:

_____

_____

_____

_____

_____

_____

_____

_____

_____

_____

_____

_____

_____

_____

_____

 Wondering what's going on inside your uterus? If you were able to take a sneak peak inside the uterus, you'd see a process of fetal development like what's re-created in the *First 9 Months* video available for viewing at Parentsplace.com Here's the link: www.parentsplace.com/first9months/main.html.

Prenatal Visit 3

Stats and Test Results

Use this page to record the stats and test results from this prenatal visit.

Date and time of visit: _____

Weight: _____

Blood pressure: _____

Pulse: _____

Urinalysis results: _____

Fetal heart rate: _____

Fundal height: _____

Other test results: _____

Going Forward

Recommendations and advice from your caregiver:

_____

_____

_____

_____

_____

_____

_____

_____

_____

_____

_____

_____

Prenatal Visit 4

Q&A
Questions to ask your doctor or midwife:

_____

_____

_____

_____

_____

_____

_____

_____

_____

_____

_____

_____

_____

_____

_____

_____

_____

 Round ligament pain (knife-like pain in your lower abdomen caused by the sudden stretching of ligaments that attach your uterus to your pelvis) tends to be at its worst between the 14th and 20th weeks of pregnancy, when your uterus is heavy enough to exert pressure on the ligaments and yet not large enough to rest any of its weight on the pelvic bones (something that happens after the 20th week).

Prenatal Visit 4

Stats and Test Results

Use this page to record the stats and test results from this prenatal visit.

Date and time of visit: _____

Weight: _____

Blood pressure: _____

Pulse: _____

Urinalysis results: _____

Fetal heart rate: _____

Fundal height: _____

Other test results: _____

Going Forward

Recommendations and advice from your caregiver:

_____

_____

_____

_____

_____

_____

_____

_____

_____

_____

_____

Prenatal Visit 5

Q&A
Questions to ask your doctor or midwife:

_____

_____

_____

_____

_____

_____

_____

_____

_____

_____

_____

_____

_____

_____

_____

_____

_____

_____

 Wondering about the technology behind obstetric ultrasounds? The Obstetric Ultrasound Web site explains how ultrasounds work. The site also features a detailed gallery of ultrasound images featuring babies at various stages of fetal development. Check out the site at www.ob-ultrasound.net.

Prenatal Visit 5

Stats and Test Results

Use this page to record the stats and test results from this prenatal visit.

Date and time of visit: _____

Weight: _____

Blood pressure: _____

Pulse: _____

Urinalysis results: _____

Fetal heart rate: _____

Fundal height: _____

Other test results: _____

Going Forward

Recommendations and advice from your caregiver:

_____

_____

_____

_____

_____

_____

_____

_____

_____

_____

_____

Prenatal Visit 6

Q&A

Questions to ask your doctor or midwife:

_____

_____

_____

_____

_____

_____

_____

_____

_____

_____

_____

_____

_____

_____

_____

_____

_____

_____

 Most caregivers want to hear about any falls you experience after the 24th week, particularly ones that result in pain or bleeding or direct blows to the abdomen. Odds are, your baby is fine, but your doctor or midwife may want to monitor the fetal heart rate and/or to do a blood test to check for bleeding from the baby's circulation to yours via the placenta. In most cases, these tests will help to reassure both of you that the baby wasn't injured.

Prenatal Visit 6

Stats and Test Results

Use this page to record the stats and test results from this prenatal visit.

Date and time of visit: _____

Weight: _____

Blood pressure: _____

Pulse: _____

Urinalysis results: _____

Fetal heart rate: _____

Fundal height: _____

Other test results: _____

Going Forward

Recommendations and advice from your caregiver:

_____

_____

_____

_____

_____

_____

_____

_____

_____

_____

_____

_____

Prenatal Visit 7

Q&A

Questions to ask your doctor or midwife:

_____

_____

_____

_____

_____

_____

_____

_____

_____

_____

_____

_____

_____

_____

_____

_____

_____

_____

_____

 A number of doctors routinely screen their patients for gestational diabetes toward the end of the second trimester or the beginning of the third.

Prenatal Visit 7

Stats and Test Results

Use this page to record the stats and test results from this prenatal visit.

Date and time of visit: _____

Weight: _____

Blood pressure: _____

Pulse: _____

Urinalysis results: _____

Fetal heart rate: _____

Fundal height: _____

Other test results: _____

Going Forward

Recommendations and advice from your caregiver:

_____

_____

_____

_____

_____

_____

_____

_____

_____

_____

_____

Prenatal Visit 8

Q&A
Questions to ask your doctor or midwife:

_____

_____

_____

_____

_____

_____

_____

_____

_____

_____

_____

_____

_____

_____

_____

_____

_____

_____

_____

_____

_____

 Studies have shown that babies are rocked to sleep by their mothers' movements during the day, and therefore tend to be most active between 8:00 p.m. and 8:00 a.m.

Prenatal Visit 8

Stats and Test Results

Use this page to record the stats and test results from this prenatal visit.

Date and time of visit: _____

Weight: _____

Blood pressure: _____

Pulse: _____

Urinalysis results: _____

Fetal heart rate: _____

Fundal height: _____

Other test results: _____

Going Forward

Recommendations and advice from your caregiver:

_____

_____

_____

_____

_____

_____

_____

_____

_____

_____

_____

Prenatal Visit 9

Q&A

Questions to ask your doctor or midwife:

_____

_____

_____

_____

_____

_____

_____

_____

_____

_____

_____

_____

_____

_____

_____

_____

_____

_____

_____

 Your baby's lungs and digestive tract are almost mature. Due to cramped conditions in the uterus, its movements may be less noticeable than they've been in recent weeks, although you should still be able to detect fetal movement on a regular basis.

Prenatal Visit 9

Stats and Test Results

Use this page to record the stats and test results from this prenatal visit.

Date and time of visit: _____

Weight: _____

Blood pressure: _____

Pulse: _____

Urinalysis results: _____

Fetal heart rate: _____

Fundal height: _____

Other test results: _____

Going Forward

Recommendations and advice from your caregiver:

_____

_____

_____

_____

_____

_____

_____

_____

_____

_____

_____

Prenatal Visit 10

Q&A
Questions to ask your doctor or midwife:

_____

_____

_____

_____

_____

_____

_____

_____

_____

_____

_____

_____

_____

_____

_____

_____

_____

 Your baby is now approximately 19 inches long — nearly its full length — and weighs approximately 4½ pounds. Throughout the next few weeks, the baby gains weight at a rapid rate, depositing layers of fat under the skin so that it will have some built-in insulation to help keep itself warm after birth.

Prenatal Visit 10

Stats and Test Results

Use this page to record the stats and test results from this prenatal visit.

Date and time of visit: _____

Weight: _____

Blood pressure: _____

Pulse: _____

Urinalysis results: _____

Fetal heart rate: _____

Fundal height: _____

Other test results: _____

Going Forward

Recommendations and advice from your caregiver:

_____

_____

_____

_____

_____

_____

_____

_____

_____

_____

_____

_____

Prenatal Visit 11

Q&A

Questions to ask your doctor or midwife:

_____

_____

_____

_____

_____

_____

_____

_____

_____

_____

_____

_____

_____

_____

_____

_____

_____

_____

 "The Top Ten Labor-Related Worries" offers reassuring words about the worries that may be running through your mind as you head into the home stretch of pregnancy. You can download your copy from www.pregnancylibrary.com.

Prenatal Visit 11

Stats and Test Results

Use this page to record the stats and test results from this prenatal visit.

Date and time of visit: _____

Weight: _____

Blood pressure: _____

Pulse: _____

Urinalysis results: _____

Fetal heart rate: _____

Fundal height: _____

Other test results: _____

Going Forward

Recommendations and advice from your caregiver:

_____

_____

_____

_____

_____

_____

_____

_____

_____

_____

_____

Prenatal Visit 12

Q&A
Questions to ask your doctor or midwife:

_____

_____

_____

_____

_____

_____

_____

_____

_____

_____

_____

_____

_____

_____

_____

_____

_____

 Don't forget to ask other new parents to pass along the names of all the best pediatricians in your area. With any luck, you'll be able to access some of these healthcare providers through your health insurance provider.

Prenatal Visit 12

Stats and Test Results

Use this page to record the stats and test results from this prenatal visit.

Date and time of visit: _____

Weight: _____

Blood pressure: _____

Pulse: _____

Urinalysis results: _____

Fetal heart rate: _____

Fundal height: _____

Other test results: _____

Going Forward

Recommendations and advice from your caregiver:

_____

_____

_____

_____

_____

_____

_____

_____

_____

_____

_____

_____

Prenatal Visit 13

Q&A
Questions to ask your doctor or midwife:

_____

_____

_____

_____

_____

_____

_____

_____

_____

_____

_____

_____

_____

_____

_____

_____

_____

_____

 The rapid period of weight gain continues, with the baby gaining approximately 1% of its body weight each day. (A 150-pound woman gaining weight at the same rate would be packing on a mind-boggling 10$\frac{1}{2}$ pounds per week!)

Prenatal Visit 13

Stats and Test Results
Use this page to record the stats and test results from this prenatal visit.

Date and time of visit: _____

Weight: _____

Blood pressure: _____

Pulse: _____

Urinalysis results: _____

Fetal heart rate: _____

Fundal height: _____

Other test results: _____

Going Forward
Recommendations and advice from your caregiver:

_____

_____

_____

_____

_____

_____

_____

_____

_____

_____

_____

Prenatal Visit 14

Q&A
Questions to ask your doctor or midwife:

_____

_____

_____

_____

_____

_____

_____

_____

_____

_____

_____

_____

_____

_____

_____

_____

The irregular contractions that occur during the last half of pregnancy are called Braxton Hicks contractions. Typically lasting for 45 seconds or less, they feel as if someone has momentarily put a blood pressure cuff around your abdomen and then pumped it up. Toward the end of pregnancy, they become increasingly uncomfortable and sometimes even painful. In fact, some women have such powerful Braxton Hicks contractions that they have a hard time distinguishing them from "the real thing."

Prenatal Visit 14

Stats and Test Results
Use this page to record the stats and test results from this prenatal visit.

Date and time of visit: _____

Weight: _____

Blood pressure: _____

Pulse: _____

Urinalysis results: _____

Fetal heart rate: _____

Fundal height: _____

Other test results: _____

Going Forward
Rocommendations and advice from your caregiver:

_____

_____

_____

_____

_____

_____

_____

_____

_____

_____

_____

Prenatal Visit 15

Q&A
Questions to ask your doctor or midwife:

_____

_____

_____

_____

_____

_____

_____

_____

_____

_____

_____

_____

_____

_____

_____

_____

 Wondering when to expect your first post-baby period? Unless you have a crystal ball, you're going to have a bit of trouble pinpointing the exact date of its arrival. While bottle-feeding mothers typically start menstruating within 6 to 8 weeks of the delivery, breastfeeding mothers can expect to get their periods back any time between 2 and 18 months after the birth.

Prenatal Visit 15

Stats and Test Results

Use this page to record the stats and test results from this prenatal visit.

Date and time of visit: _____

Weight: _____

Blood pressure: _____

Pulse: _____

Urinalysis results: _____

Fetal heart rate: _____

Fundal height: _____

Other test results: _____

Going Forward

Recommendations and advice from your caregiver:

_____

_____

_____

_____

_____

_____

_____

_____

_____

_____

_____

Exercising During Pregnancy

Although there's nothing you can really do to "train" for labor, studies have shown that your labor is likely to be shorter and less complicated if you're in good physical condition when those first contractions hit. That's why most pregnant women are encouraged to make exercise part of their regular routine. Your goal, however, should be to maintain your current level of physical conditioning during pregnancy — not to embark on a heavy-duty training program.

Assuming you do get the go-ahead from your caregiver, it's still necessary to proceed with caution. Here are some important points to keep in mind when you're planning your fitness program:

✎ **Choose your fitness activity with care.** Avoid anything that could leave you susceptible to injury — deep knee bends, full sit-ups, double-leg raises, straight-leg raises, and so on. You can also reduce the risk of injury by incorporating a warm-up and a cool-down into your workout.

✎ **Avoid activities that could result in abdominal trauma or other types of injuries.** Your best bets are walking, swimming and water aerobics, stationary cycling, and low-impact aerobics. Activities that aren't usually recommended include contact sports such as football, basketball, and volleyball; adventure sports such as parachuting, mountain climbing, and scuba diving; sports with a high risk of trauma, such as downhill skiing, horseback riding, water-skiing, surfing, and ice skating; and high-impact, weight-bearing sports such as running or jogging.

✎ **Avoid exercising in the tilted supine (semi-reclined) position.**

✎ **Keep in mind that you'll probably tire more easily than usual.**

✎ **Don't overexert yourself.**

✎ **Don't allow your body to become overheated.**

Exercising During Pregnancy

/ Consume enough liquids to keep yourself well hydrated.

/ Make sure that you're eating enough.

/ If you start feeling winded or shaky, if you experience vaginal bleeding or uterine contractions, or if your membranes rupture, stop exercising immediately.

/ Avoid exercising on your back after the 20th week of pregnancy.

/ **Have fun!** Sign up for a prenatal fitness class so that you can get to know other pregnant women in your community. Hop on your stationary bike while you're reading your favorite pregnancy magazine. And make an after-dinner stroll with your partner part of your daily routine.

Floor exercises are simple activities that prepare you for labor. Consider doing these exercises even if you don't feel up for any other activity.

Type of Exercise	What It Does for You
Squatting	Stretches the legs and opens the pelvis; great preparation for birth if you intend to do some of your laboring and birthing in a squatting position
Pelvic tilting	Strengthens the muscles in your abdomen and back to improve your overall posture and prevent or relieve backache
Abdominal curl-ups	Strengthens the abdominal muscles that support the uterus
Pelvic floor exercises	Strengthens the muscles that support the abdominal organs; helps to prevent pregnancy incontinence; can make birth easier

Quick Index to Your Medications

Use these pages to keep track of all medications you're taking — both over-the-counter and prescription products. For each medication, indicate the name of the drug, who prescribed it, its indication (what condition the drug treats), instructions for taking the medication, any warning signs described by your physician, and possible side effects.

Drug: _____
Physician: _____
Indication: _____
Instructions: _____
_____
Warnings and possible side effects: _____
_____
_____
_____
_____

Drug: _____
Physician: _____
Indication: _____
Instructions: _____
_____
Warnings and possible side effects: _____
_____
_____
_____
_____

Quick Index to Your Medications

Drug: _____
Physician: _____
Indication: _____
Instructions: _____
_____
Warnings and possible side effects: _____
_____
_____
_____

Drug: _____
Physician: _____
Indication: _____
Instructions: _____
_____
Warnings and possible side effects: _____
_____
_____
_____

Drug: _____
Physician: _____
Indication: _____
Instructions: _____
_____
Warnings and possible side effects: _____
_____
_____
_____
_____

Quick Index to Your Medications

Drug: _____
Physician: _____
Indication: _____
Instructions: _____
_____
Warnings and possible side effects: _____
_____
_____
_____

Drug: _____
Physician: _____
Indication: _____
Instructions: _____
_____
Warnings and possible side effects: _____
_____
_____
_____

Drug: _____
Physician: _____
Indication: _____
Instructions: _____
_____
Warnings and possible side effects: _____
_____
_____
_____
_____

Quick Index to Your Medications

Drug: _____

Physician: _____

Indication: _____

Instructions: _____

_____

Warnings and possible side effects: _____

_____

_____

_____

Drug: _____

Physician: _____

Indication: _____

Instructions: _____

_____

Warnings and possible side effects: _____

_____

_____

_____

Drug: _____

Physician: _____

Indication: _____

Instructions: _____

_____

Warnings and possible side effects: _____

_____

_____

_____

_____

Notes

Notes

Notes

Your Weekly Planner

Your Weekly Planner

Every week of your pregnancy is filled with unique experiences. There will be times when you're so full of energy that you seriously question whether this pregnancy thing is actually for real — and other times when you can barely muster up the strength to drag yourself from the couch to your bed after a pre-bedtime siesta. (The sleep experts may not approve, but sometimes it's all you can do to keep your eyes open between dinner and bedtime!)

And then there are those much-talked-about pregnancy food cravings — sudden cravings for foods you might not normally even bother with. (Of course, the jury's still out on whether pregnancy food cravings even exist — an interesting topic for debate at your next childbirth class!)

You'll also find space in this part of the organizer to record details about some of the classic pregnancy complaints: nausea, round ligament pain, and back pain, to name but a few. (You'll look back fondly on this stuff in years to come. Really.)

You won't find out you're pregnant until Week 3 at the earliest, even if your doctor does a blood test. (Most home pregnancy tests are accurate sometime between 10 to 14 days post-ovulation — around the middle or end of Week 3, but a blood test may be able to give you an accurate result a little sooner.)

It may seem odd to be officially three or four weeks pregnant the moment the pregnancy test comes back positive, but it will all make sense if you remember that your doctor or midwife dates your pregnancy by counting back to the first day of your last menstrual period — something that happens two weeks prior to ovulation if you have a classic 28-day menstrual cycle.

Whenever you begin this journal, whether it's during Week 3 or Week 8, make a point of going back and reconstructing the early weeks of your pregnancy as best you can. Knowing as much as possible about the early weeks of your pregnancy can help your caregiver date your pregnancy more accurately, plus you'll have a record of these all too easy-to-forget details, whether as a memento for yourself or as a reference for a subsequent pregnancy.

Also use these weekly planner pages to jot down your memorable moments, including baby kicks and other movements, test results that put your mind at ease, great advice from family and friends (the only advice that's worth paying attention to, by the way!), and anything else that you want to remember.

The Complaint Department

While there's no such thing as a one-size-fits-all pregnancy, certain complaints tend to be more of a problem during certain trimesters.

Pregnancy-Related Complaint	Month During Pregnancy When It's Most Likely to Be a Problem								
	1	2	3	4	5	6	7	8	9
Abdominal muscle separation				X	X	X	X	X	X
Acne	X	X	X	X	X	X	X	X	X
Backache							X	X	X
Belly button soreness				X					
Bleeding gums (pregnancy gingivitis)	X	X	X	X	X	X	X	X	X
Bleeding or spotting	X	X	X						
Braxton Hicks contractions						X	X	X	X
Breast enlargement	X	X	X	X	X	X	X	X	X
Breast tenderness	X	X	X						
Breathlessness							X	X	
Carpal tunnel syndrome				X	X	X	X	X	X
Constipation	X	X	X	X	X	X	X	X	X
Cramping (abdominal)	X								
Cravings	X	X	X						
Edema (fluid retention) and swelling							X	X	X
Eye changes (dryness vision changes)	X	X	X	X	X	X	X	X	X
Faintness and dizziness	X	X	X	X	X	X	X	X	X
Fatigue	X	X	X				X	X	X
Food aversions	X	X	X	X	X	X	X	X	X
Gas and bloating	X	X	X	X	X	X	X	X	X
Headaches	X	X	X	X	X	X	X	X	X
Heartburn							X	X	X
Hemorrhoids				X	X	X	X	X	X

The Complaint Department

Pregnancy-Related Complaint	Month During Pregnancy When It's Most Likely to Be a Problem								
	1	2	3	4	5	6	7	8	9
Hip soreness				X	X	X	X	X	X
Insomnia	X	X	X	X	X	X	X	X	X
Itchiness		X					X	X	X
Leg cramps							X	X	X
Linea nigra (vertical line center of abdomen)				X	X	X	X	X	X
Mask of pregnancy (chloasma)				X	X	X	X	X	X
Morning sickness	X	X	X						
Perineal aching									X
Pubic bone pain				X	X	X	X	X	X
Rashes							X	X	X
Rhinitis	X	X	X	X	X	X	X	X	X
Round ligament pain				X	X				
Sciatica							X	X	X
Skin changes	X	X	X	X	X	X	X	X	X
Smell, heightened sense of	X	X	X						
Stretch marks							X	X	X
Sweating, increased				X	X	X	X	X	X
Swelling and edema (fluid retention)							X	X	X
Thirstiness	X	X	X	X	X	X	X	X	X
Urinary incontinence (leaking of urine)							X	X	X
Urination, increased frequency	X	X	X				X	X	X
Vaginal discharge, increased	X	X	X	X	X	X	X	X	X
Varicose veins							X	X	X
Weepiness	X	X	X	X	X	X	X	X	X
Yeast infections	X	X	X	X	X	X	X	X	X

Week 3

Mood: _____

_____

Energy level: _____

_____

Comfort level: _____

_____

Appetite/cravings: _____

_____

_____

Nausea or vomiting (morning sickness): _____

_____

Fitness activity this week: _____

_____

_____

This week . . . _____

_____

_____

_____

_____

_____

_____

_____

_____

_____

Week 3

According to the American Academy of Pediatrics, fewer than one in three pregnant American women consumes enough folic acid. The U.S. Public Health Service and Health Canada recommend that, as early as possible (ideally, prior to becoming pregnant), you take at least 0.4 mg of folic acid per day. Some conditions may require more folic acid each day — ask your caregiver for details.

Memorable Moments This Week

Week 4

Mood: _____

_____

Energy level: _____

Comfort level: _____

Appetite/cravings: _____

_____

Nausea or vomiting (morning sickness): _____

_____

Fitness activity this week: _____

_____

This week . . . _____

_____

_____

_____

_____

_____

_____

_____

_____

_____

Week 4

Don't be surprised if you experience some period-like cramping around the time your first missed menstrual period was due. This cramping is simply the body's response to the hormonal changes of early pregnancy. As long as it isn't accompanied by bleeding (one of the warning signs of miscarriage) or sharp pain limited to one side of your abdomen (one of the warning signs of an ectopic pregnancy), there's generally no cause for concern.

_____

_____

_____

_____

_____

Memorable Moments This Week

_____

_____

_____

_____

_____

_____

_____

_____

_____

_____

Week 5

Mood: _____
_____

Energy level: _____
_____

Comfort level: _____
_____

Appetite/cravings: _____
_____
_____

Nausea or vomiting (morning sickness): _____
_____

Fitness activity this week: _____
_____
_____

This week . . . _____
_____
_____
_____
_____
_____
_____
_____
_____
_____

Week 5

This week, the hands have started to appear and major organs are now being formed. Your baby is now the size of an apple seed. Within another week, the heart will begin to beat, and other major organs such as the kidneys and the liver will start to develop.

Memorable Moments This Week

Week 6

Mood: _____

_____

Energy level: _____

_____

Comfort level: _____

_____

Appetite/cravings: _____

_____

_____

Nausea or vomiting (morning sickness): _____

_____

Fitness activity this week: _____

_____

_____

This week . . . _____

_____

_____

_____

_____

_____

_____

_____

_____

_____

_____

_____

Week 6

Looking for a reason to get off the couch and hit the gym? Pregnant women who exercise three or four times a week have the best chance of giving birth to a healthy-weight baby.

Memorable Moments This Week

Week 7

Mood: _____

_____

Energy level: _____

_____

Comfort level: _____

_____

Appetite/cravings: _____

_____

_____

Nausea or vomiting (morning sickness): _____

_____

Fitness activity this week: _____

_____

_____

This week . . . _____

_____

_____

_____

_____

_____

_____

_____

_____

_____

Week 7

Your baby's eyes continue to form and begin to develop pigment. Fingers, toes, and outer ears begin to take shape. Your baby is now approximately 1 inch long!

Memorable Moments This Week

Week 8

Mood: _____

_____

Energy level: _____

_____

Comfort level: _____

_____

Appetite/cravings: _____

_____

_____

Nausea or vomiting (morning sickness): _____

_____

Fitness activity this week: _____

_____

_____

This week . . . _____

_____

_____

_____

_____

_____

_____

_____

_____

_____

Week 8

Ideally, you should aim for a slow, steady weight gain. While you're not likely to gain much weight at all during the first trimester — most women tend to gain somewhere between two and eight pounds — you should expect to continue to gain weight at a more rapid rate during the second and third trimesters. Your weight gain will, however, tend to taper off during the last week or two of pregnancy, as your body begins to prepare for the birth.

Memorable Moments This Week

Week 9

Mood: _____

_____

Energy level: _____

Comfort level: _____

Appetite/cravings: _____

_____

_____

Nausea or vomiting (morning sickness): _____

_____

Fitness activity this week: _____

_____

_____

This week . . . _____

_____

_____

_____

_____

_____

_____

_____

_____

Week 9

You can probably get away with wearing most of your regular clothes until at least the start of the second trimester, although you may have to bid a temporary farewell to your dress pants and fitted skirts a little sooner than that.

_____
_____
_____
_____
_____
_____
_____

Memorable Moments This Week

_____
_____
_____
_____
_____
_____
_____
_____
_____
_____

Week 10

Mood: _____

_____

Energy level: _____

_____

Comfort level: _____

_____

Appetite/cravings: _____

_____

_____

Nausea or vomiting (morning sickness): _____

_____

Fitness activity this week: _____

_____

_____

This week . . . _____

_____

_____

_____

_____

_____

_____

_____

_____

_____

Week 10

Your risk of experiencing a miscarriage drops dramatically after your doctor or midwife is able to pick up your baby's heartbeat via ultrasound or Doppler (a hand-held ultrasound device that can usually pick up the baby's heartbeat by the start of the second trimester). One study showed that your risk of experiencing a miscarriage drops to less than two percent if your baby's heartbeat is detected when you're ten weeks pregnant.

Memorable Moments This Week

Week 11

Mood: _____

_____

Energy level: _____

_____

Comfort level: _____

_____

Appetite/cravings: _____

_____

_____

Nausea or vomiting (morning sickness): _____

_____

Fitness activity this week: _____

_____

_____

This week . . . _____

_____

_____

_____

_____

_____

_____

_____

_____

_____

Week 11

Your baby's head now makes up approximately half of its length. While the ovaries and testicles are fully formed and the external genitalia are developing, it's still too early to distinguish the sex. The baby is now about 2 inches long and weighs approximately half an ounce.

_____
_____
_____
_____
_____
_____
_____

Memorable Moments This Week

_____
_____
_____
_____
_____
_____
_____
_____
_____
_____

Week 12

Mood: _____

_____

Energy level: _____

_____

Comfort level: _____

_____

Appetite/cravings: _____

_____

_____

Nausea or vomiting (morning sickness): _____

_____

Fitness activity this week: _____

_____

_____

This week . . . _____

_____

_____

_____

_____

_____

_____

_____

_____

_____

Week 12

Looking for the lowdown on nutrition during pregnancy? The Tufts Nutrition Navigator can help to find your way to the best nutrition Web sites — the ones packed with scientifically sound, need-to-know information. You can find the Nutrition Navigator Online at www.navigator.tufts.edu.

Memorable Moments This Week

Week 13

Mood: _____
_____

Energy level: _____
_____

Comfort level: _____
_____

Appetite/cravings: _____
_____
_____

Nausea or vomiting (morning sickness): _____
_____

Fitness activity this week: _____
_____
_____

This week . . . _____
_____
_____
_____
_____
_____
_____
_____
_____
_____
_____

Week 13

This is the week when your baby's intestines migrate from the umbilical cord into the abdomen. The eyes and ears have almost moved into their permanent position, and the baby has already acquired some rudimentary reflexes.

_____

_____

_____

_____

_____

_____

Memorable Moments This Week

_____

_____

_____

_____

_____

_____

_____

_____

Week 14

Mood: _____

_____

Energy level: _____

_____

Comfort level: _____

_____

Appetite/cravings: _____

_____

_____

Nausea or vomiting (morning sickness): _____

_____

Fitness activity this week: _____

_____

_____

This week . . . _____

_____

_____

_____

_____

_____

_____

_____

_____

_____

_____

Week 14

 Right around this week, your pregnancy symptoms might have sponta-
neously disappeared. This typically — and thankfully for mothers who
have experienced extreme morning sickness — happens at the end of
the first trimester. For approximately the next three months, you
should be feeling wonderful!

_____

_____

_____

_____

_____

Memorable Moments This Week

_____

_____

_____

_____

_____

_____

_____

_____

_____

_____

Week 15

Mood: _____

_____

Energy level: _____

_____

Comfort level: _____

_____

Appetite/cravings: _____

_____

_____

Fitness activity this week: _____

_____

_____

This week . . . _____

_____

_____

_____

_____

_____

_____

_____

_____

_____

_____

_____

_____

Week 15

Wondering what you can do to increase your odds of giving birth to a healthy baby? The March of Dimes Web site (www.modimes.org) is an excellent source of information on everything from preventing birth defects to minimizing the risk of preterm labor.

_____

_____

_____

_____

_____

_____

_____

Memorable Moments This Week

_____

_____

_____

_____

_____

_____

_____

_____

_____

Week 16

Mood: _____

Energy level: _____

Comfort level: _____

Appetite/cravings: _____

_____

Fitness activity this week: _____

_____

This week . . . _____

_____

_____

_____

_____

_____

_____

_____

_____

_____

_____

Week 16

Your baby's joints are now fully functional. At some point over the next four weeks, you'll likely feel its kicks for the very first time. These early kicks are very subtle, often described as butterflies in the stomach.

Memorable Moments This Week

Week 17

Mood: _____

_____

Energy level: _____

_____

Comfort level: _____

_____

Appetite/cravings: _____

_____

_____

Fitness activity this week: _____

_____

_____

This week . . . _____

_____

_____

_____

_____

_____

_____

_____

_____

_____

_____

_____

Week 17

 Now is the time for a quick getaway with your partner. By 25 weeks, you'll want to begin curtailing your travel plans to only those areas that have excellent newborn healthcare facilities. By 32 to 36 weeks, according to airline regulations, you won't be able to travel by airplane within the country, and deadlines for foreign air travel may be even earlier. Besides, you're likely feeling very energetic and healthy at this point; take advantage of your urge to travel while it lasts!

_____

_____

_____

_____

_____

Memorable Moments This Week

_____

_____

_____

_____

_____

_____

_____

_____

_____

_____

Week 18

Mood: _____

_____

Energy level: _____

_____

Comfort level: _____

_____

Appetite/cravings: _____

_____

_____

Baby movements: _____

_____

_____

Fitness activity this week: _____

_____

_____

This week . . . _____

_____

_____

_____

_____

_____

_____

_____

_____

Week 18

That garage-sale bargain may not seem like such a great deal if you later discover that the crib or stroller your purchased has been pulled off the market by the U.S. Consumer Product Safety Commissions or Health Canada. So do your homework before you hit the garage-sale circuit by reading up on product safety recalls at the CPSC Web site: www.cpsc.gov or at the Health Canada Web site: www.hc-sc.gc.ca.

_____

_____

_____

_____

_____

_____

Memorable Moments This Week

_____

_____

_____

_____

_____

_____

_____

_____

_____

_____

Week 19

Mood: _____

_____

Energy level: _____

_____

Comfort level: _____

_____

Appetite/cravings: _____

_____

_____

Baby movements: _____

_____

_____

Fitness activity this week: _____

_____

_____

This week . . . _____

_____

_____

_____

_____

_____

_____

_____

_____

Week 19

If you're planning to return to work after the birth of your baby, start giving serious thought to your childcare options by the time you head into your third trimester of pregnancy. And if you're counting on landing an infant space in one of the crème de la crème daycare centers, you may want to get your name on the waiting list even sooner than that — perhaps the moment the pregnancy test comes back positive!

Memorable Moments This Week

Week 20

Mood: _____

_____

Energy level: _____

_____

Comfort level: _____

_____

Appetite/cravings: _____

_____

_____

Baby movements: _____

_____

_____

Fitness activity this week: _____

_____

_____

This week . . . _____

_____

_____

_____

_____

_____

_____

_____

_____

Week 20

Your baby's senses of taste and smell are fully developed. The baby is now approximately 6¹⁄₂ inches long and weighs about 9 ounces.

Memorable Moments This Week

Week 21

Mood: _____

_____

Energy level: _____

_____

Comfort level: _____

_____

Appetite/cravings: _____

_____

_____

Baby movements: _____

_____

_____

Fitness activity this week: _____

_____

_____

This week . . . _____

_____

_____

_____

_____

_____

_____

_____

_____

_____

Week 21

The point at which the first flutters and kicks can be detected varies considerably from woman to woman and from pregnancy to pregnancy, but they're typically felt sometime between the 18th and 22nd weeks of pregnancy.

Memorable Moments This Week

Week 22

Mood: _____

_____

Energy level: _____

_____

Comfort level: _____

_____

Appetite/cravings: _____

_____

_____

Baby movements: _____

_____

_____

Fitness activity this week: _____

_____

_____

This week . . . _____

_____

_____

_____

_____

_____

_____

_____

_____

Week 22

Your baby's skin is sensitive to touch, and the baby will often respond when pressure is placed on your abdomen. By this stage of pregnancy, the fingernails have been formed and the eyebrows and eyelids are fully developed. The baby is now approximately $7^1/_2$ inches long and weighs approximately $^3/_4$ of a pound.

_____

_____

_____

_____

_____

_____

_____

Memorable Moments This Week

_____

_____

_____

_____

_____

_____

_____

_____

_____

_____

Week 23

Mood: _____

_____

Energy level: _____

Comfort level: _____

Appetite/cravings: _____

_____

Baby movements: _____

_____

Fitness activity this week: _____

_____

This week . . . _____

_____

_____

_____

_____

_____

_____

_____

Week 23

Memorable Moments This Week

Week 24

Mood: _____

_____

Energy level: _____

_____

Comfort level: _____

_____

Appetite/cravings: _____

_____

_____

Baby movements: _____

_____

_____

Fitness activity this week: _____

_____

_____

This week . . . _____

_____

_____

_____

_____

_____

_____

_____

_____

Week 24

Don't expect your partner to be able to feel your baby's kicks until toward the end of your second trimester. It's only after about Week 24 that those kicks will be strong enough to be felt by anyone but you.

_____

_____

_____

_____

_____

_____

_____

_____

Memorable Moments This Week

_____

_____

_____

_____

_____

_____

_____

_____

_____

Week 25

Mood: _____

_____

Energy level: _____

_____

Comfort level: _____

_____

Appetite/cravings: _____

_____

_____

Baby movements: _____

_____

_____

Fitness activity this week: _____

_____

_____

This week . . . _____

_____

_____

_____

_____

_____

_____

_____

_____

_____

Week 25

Your baby regularly experiences episodes of hiccupping during the second half of pregnancy. It is now approximately 9 inches long and weighs approximately 1½ pounds.

Memorable Moments This Week

Week 26

Mood: _____

_____

Energy level: _____

_____

Comfort level: _____

_____

Appetite/cravings: _____

_____

_____

Baby movements: _____

_____

_____

Fitness activity this week: _____

_____

_____

This week . . . _____

_____

_____

_____

_____

_____

_____

_____

_____

_____

Week 26

Your baby has developed distinct periods of sleeping and waking, and its brain patterns now resemble those of a newborn baby.

_____

_____

_____

_____

_____

_____

_____

Memorable Moments This Week

_____

_____

_____

_____

_____

_____

_____

_____

_____

_____

Week 27

Mood: _____

Energy level: _____

Comfort level: _____

Appetite/cravings: _____
_____

Baby movements: _____
_____

Fitness activity this week: _____
_____

This week . . . _____
_____
_____
_____
_____
_____
_____
_____
_____

Week 27

> ☼ Wondering what your childbirth instructor won't tell you about giving birth? Get the lowdown by reading "Ten Things Your Prenatal Instructor Won't Tell You" at www.pregnancylibrary.com.

_____

_____

_____

_____

_____

_____

_____

Memorable Moments This Week

_____

_____

_____

_____

_____

_____

_____

_____

_____

Week 28

Mood: _____

_____

Energy level: _____

_____

Comfort level: _____

_____

Appetite/cravings: _____

_____

_____

Baby movements: _____

_____

_____

Fitness activity this week: _____

_____

_____

This week . . . _____

_____

_____

_____

_____

_____

_____

_____

_____

_____

Week 28

Your baby is between 12 and 15 inches long and weighs approximately 2½ to 3 pounds.

_____

_____

_____

_____

_____

_____

_____

_____

Memorable Moments This Week

_____

_____

_____

_____

_____

_____

_____

_____

Week 29

Mood: _____
_____

Energy level: _____
_____

Comfort level: _____
_____

Appetite/cravings: _____
_____
_____

Baby movements: _____
_____
_____

Fitness activity this week: _____
_____
_____

This week . . . _____
_____
_____
_____
_____
_____
_____
_____
_____

Week 29

An old wives' tale says that a pregnant woman who frequently gets heartburn will have a baby who's born with a full head of hair. While that's not true, heartburn is a common side effect of pregnancy. To minimize your heartburn problems, eat several small meals throughout the day, avoid spicy and fried foods, and drink a glass of milk before you eat.

Memorable Moments This Week

Week 30

Mood: _____

_____

Energy level: _____

_____

Comfort level: _____

_____

Appetite/cravings: _____

_____

_____

Baby movements: _____

_____

_____

Fitness activity this week: _____

_____

_____

This week . . . _____

_____

_____

_____

_____

_____

_____

_____

_____

Week 30

Much of the stress of pregnancy comes from being unsure about what's normal and what's not during this weird yet wonderful time in your life. In addition to turning to your doctor or midwife for support and information, you may want to line up a pregnancy mentor — a woman who is either pregnant herself (ideally a few months ahead of you) or who has recently given birth. To find yourself a mentor, just swap phone numbers and e-mail addresses with someone you're comfortable with and who is willing to share her experiences with you. Having someone to turn to for from-the-trenches advice can help to alleviate a lot of your anxiety.

Memorable Moments This Week

Week 31

Mood: _____

_____

Energy level: _____

_____

Comfort level: _____

_____

Appetite/cravings: _____

_____

_____

Baby movements: _____

_____

_____

Fitness activity this week: _____

_____

_____

This week . . . _____

_____

_____

_____

_____

_____

_____

_____

_____

Week 31

Finding it hard to get the sleep you're so desperately craving? Check out "Will the Sandman Ever Come? Pregnancy and Sleep" from www.pregnancylibrary.com for some practical strategies on doing battle with pregnancy-related insomnia.

_____

_____

_____

_____

_____

_____

_____

Memorable Moments This Week

_____

_____

_____

_____

_____

_____

_____

_____

_____

Week 32

Mood: _____

_____

Energy level: _____

Comfort level: _____

Appetite/cravings: _____

_____

Baby movements: _____

_____

Fitness activity this week: _____

_____

This week . . . _____

_____

_____

_____

_____

_____

_____

_____

_____

Week 32

In your seventh or eighth month, pressure from your growing uterus makes breathing increasingly difficult. To make matters worse, high levels of progesterone leave you feeling short of breath, something that triggers the desire to breathe more deeply. You can ease the discomfort in the meantime by using an extra pillow at night, when breathlessness tends to be particularly annoying.

Memorable Moments This Week

8 Months and Counting

While you might feel as though you're in a bit of a holding pattern, as you wait for your baby to make his or her grand entrance, there's actually a lot going on inside your body. Here are just a few of the physical changes and sensations you may notice as you head into the home stretch:

- Your baby may be doing fewer somersaults than she was a few weeks ago. The reason is obvious: Conditions inside the uterus are getting a little cramped.

- You may be experiencing a lot of pain underneath your ribs.

- You may feel some sudden, darting movements by your baby.

- You may feel as though your pelvic floor muscles are supporting a cantaloupe.

- You may feel increased pressure in your pelvis and rectum.

- You may find that your breathlessness decreases, but that annoying urge to urinate every hour on the hour returns. You may also find yourself experiencing a variety of other pregnancy complaints: sciatica, varicose veins, hemorrhoids, and stretch marks.

- Your Braxton Hicks contractions (practice contractions — not the real thing) may become increasingly uncomfortable — and perhaps even painful.

- Your eating habits may change. You may find that you need smaller, more frequent meals rather than several large meals each day.

- You may feel more — or less — energetic.

- You may lose weight.

8 Months and Counting

During the eighth and ninth months, you may also notice that your emotional state changes. Even if you've been thoroughly enjoying your pregnancy, you may now be eager to get on with the show. This whole business of being pregnant has long since lost its novelty: Now all you can think about is meeting your baby!

And then there's the business of the impending labor — something that can have you tossing and turning at 3:00 a.m., wondering what on earth you were thinking when you decided to get pregnant eight months ago. After all, the woman in the birth film they showed in prenatal class didn't exactly look like she was having fun.

As your baby's birth day approaches, you may find that you feel increasingly introspective, more tuned into what's going on with your baby and less interested in the world around you. Be sure to treasure this special time before the birth.

What's Different?

Record details of what's changing as you enter your last two months of pregnancy:

_____

_____

_____

_____

_____

_____

_____

_____

Week 33

Mood: _____

_____

Energy level: _____

_____

Comfort level: _____

_____

Appetite/cravings: _____

_____

_____

Baby movements: _____

_____

_____

Fitness activity this week: _____

_____

_____

This week . . . _____

_____

_____

_____

_____

_____

_____

_____

_____

_____

Week 33

Your baby's skull bones are not yet joined together — nor will they be until after birth. This provides some added flexibility during birth, just in case you happen to have a smaller-than-average pelvis and your baby has a bigger-than-average head.

Memorable Moments This Week

Week 34

Mood: _____

_____

Energy level: _____

_____

Comfort level: _____

_____

Appetite/cravings: _____

_____

_____

Baby movements: _____

_____

_____

Fitness activity this week: _____

_____

_____

This week . . . _____

_____

_____

_____

_____

_____

_____

_____

_____

_____

Week 34

If you're about to become a parent for the first time, this is the last time in your life that you'll be able to enjoy the luxury of being responsible only for yourself — of going to bed whenever you feel like it and sleeping in as late as you want. Indulge thyself.

Memorable Moments This Week

Week 35

Mood: _____

_____

Energy level: _____

_____

Comfort level: _____

_____

Appetite/cravings: _____

_____

_____

Baby movements: _____

_____

_____

Fitness activity this week: _____

_____

_____

This week . . . _____

_____

_____

_____

_____

_____

_____

_____

_____

Week 35

Your baby has generally settled into a head-down position by this stage of pregnancy, but it may still make a few more flip-flops before labor begins.

_____

_____

_____

_____

_____

_____

_____

_____

Memorable Moments This Week

_____

_____

_____

_____

_____

_____

_____

_____

_____

Week 36

Mood: _____

_____

Energy level: _____

_____

Comfort level: _____

_____

Appetite/cravings: _____

_____

_____

Baby movements: _____

_____

_____

Fitness activity this week: _____

_____

_____

This week . . . _____

_____

_____

_____

_____

_____

_____

_____

_____

_____

Week 36

Feel like you're carrying a bowling ball with your perineum (the area between the vagina and the rectum)? You're not alone. It's not at all unusual to experience aching, pressure, or sharp twinges in the perineal area during late pregnancy, after the baby's head has descended into the pelvis. The Kegel exercises that your prenatal instructor likes to rave about can help to strengthen your perineal muscles, readying them for the challenges of labor.

Memorable Moments This Week

Week 37

Mood: _____
_____

Energy level: _____
_____

Comfort level: _____
_____

Appetite/cravings: _____
_____
_____

Baby movements: _____
_____
_____

Fitness activity this week: _____
_____
_____

This week . . . _____
_____
_____
_____
_____
_____
_____
_____
_____

Week 37

 A common old wives' tale is that women go into labor during a full moon; many hospital nurses even claim this is true. Research doesn't bear this out, however.

_____

_____

_____

_____

_____

_____

_____

Memorable Moments This Week

_____

_____

_____

_____

_____

_____

_____

_____

_____

_____

Week 38

Mood: _____

_____

Energy level: _____

Comfort level: _____

_____

Appetite/cravings: _____

_____

_____

Baby movements: _____

_____

_____

Fitness activity this week: _____

_____

_____

This week . . . _____

_____

_____

_____

_____

_____

_____

_____

_____

_____

Week 38

 Your baby will grow at a phenomenal rate during the early weeks and months of life and will likely outgrow his entire newborn wardrobe before he's 6 weeks old! (Note: A baby who weighs in at more than nine pounds may have a hard time fitting into the 3-month size of clothing, let alone the newborn size). Be sure to have some 6 month–size clothing on hand, just in case you end up giving birth to a larger-than-average baby.

Memorable Moments This Week

Week 39

Mood: _____

_____

Energy level: _____

_____

Comfort level: _____

_____

Appetite/cravings: _____

_____

_____

Baby movements: _____

_____

_____

Contractions: _____

_____

_____

Fitness activity this week: _____

_____

_____

This week . . . _____

_____

_____

_____

_____

_____

_____

Week 39

Don't be surprised if you find yourself feeling a little faint for a day or so after the birth. Body fluid levels shift suddenly when pregnancy ends and it can take a bit of time for your cardiovascular system to adjust. It's also not unusual to experience shivers and shakes right after you've given birth. Researchers believe this occurs because of a resetting of the body's temperature-regulating system as your pregnancy comes to an end.

Memorable Moments This Week

Week 40

Mood: _____

_____

Energy level: _____

_____

Comfort level: _____

_____

Appetite/cravings: _____

_____

_____

Baby movements: _____

_____

_____

Contractions: _____

_____

_____

Fitness activity this week: _____

_____

_____

This week . . . _____

_____

_____

_____

_____

_____

_____

Week 40

Give some serious thought to post-delivery birth control. There's a very good chance that you'll ovulate before you get your first period — something you might want to bear in mind if you're not eager to see the pregnancy test come back positive again just yet.

_____

_____

_____

_____

_____

_____

_____

Memorable Moments This Week

_____

_____

_____

_____

_____

_____

_____

_____

_____

Week 41 — 1 Week Past Due

Mood: _____

_____

Energy level: _____

_____

Comfort level: _____

_____

Appetite/cravings: _____

_____

_____

Baby movements: _____

_____

_____

Contractions: _____

_____

_____

Fitness activity this week: _____

_____

_____

This week . . . _____

_____

_____

_____

_____

_____

_____

Week 41 — 1 Week Past Due

A common old wives' tale is that when a baby is born with café au lait spots (light-brown birthmarks), the mother drank too much coffee during pregnancy. Not true.

Memorable Moments This Week

Week 42 — 2 Weeks Past Due

Mood: _____

Energy level: _____

Comfort level: _____

Appetite/cravings: _____

Baby movements: _____

Contractions: _____

Fitness activity this week: _____

This week . . . _____

_____

_____

_____

_____

_____

Week 42 — 2 Weeks Past Due

 Your due date has come and gone and there's still no baby — not what you expected when you signed what you thought was a 40-week contract! Here are some tips for maintaining your sanity:

- Remember that it's perfectly normal to be overdue.
- Keep yourself busy and don't be afraid to make plans just because you may have to cancel. Having a baby is the best excuse ever for standing someone up.
- Pamper yourself. Take advantage of those last baby-free days.
- Enjoy the time alone with your partner. It may be your last for a while.

Memorable Moments This Week

Notes

Revving Up For Baby

Revving Up For Baby

Revving up for baby means shopping for or otherwise acquiring baby gear and equipment, clothes and linens, diapers, and dozens of other odds and ends. (Hint: Before you give your credit card too much of a workout, wait to see what kind of secondhand goodies may be coming your way. There may be boxes and boxes of baby stuff with your name on them sitting in friends' and relatives' basements and garages.)

Of course, you can't leave everything to chance, unless you're a bit of a risk-taker and you want to take your gambling approach to life with you into pregnancy. If you're more inclined to hedge your bets when acquiring baby gear, you may want to think about registering your baby wish list by signing up with one or more baby store gift registries so that if friends, relatives, or coworkers want to arrange a shower or send gifts, you'll increase your odds of receiving at least some of the items on your list. If you decide to register, keep in mind that you'll still need to purchase some baby essentials on your own. You don't want to get caught short when it comes to diapering supplies, for example! In this section, you find not only checklists of all the stock-up essentials you need but also space for tracking gift registries and organizing thank-you notes.

Getting ready for your new baby also means decorating your baby's room and embarking on the process of baby-proofing. Here, you find reminders about safe ways to prepare your home for your baby's arrival.

The final step in revving up for baby is choosing a pediatrician or other doctor who will care for your child in the years to come. In this section, you find a list of questions to ask a potential pediatrician, so that you can feel confident that you've managed to zero in on Dr. Right.

Baby Stock-Up Essentials

Major Baby Gear

✐ **A car seat:** Purchase a new (not secondhand) car seat and look for a model with a fully removable, washable cover. Also look for ease of use, because leaning into the car with a wiggly baby is already awkward enough.

✐ **A baby carrier:** Look for a model that's completely machine washable, provides adequate head and back support for the baby, features padded leg holes that are roomy enough to keep your baby from sliding out and yet not so small that they are tight and uncomfortable for your baby, has padded and adjustable shoulder straps, and is easy to get on and off.

✐ **A stroller:** Make sure the model you choose is easy to steer and easy to fold. Also, look for these features: a strong but lightweight aluminum frame; a broad base and stable design; stain-resistant fabric; a sun and rain shield; lockable wheels; secure and easy-to-use restraining straps; a removable front bar; an adjustable footrest; a reversible and adjustable handle; and storage space under the seat.

✐ **A bassinet, cradle, or crib:** Decide whether you even need a bassinet or cradle, or whether a crib will suffice. When purchasing a crib, look for a firm, tight-fitting mattress, no loose or missing hardware or crib slats, no more than 2⅜ inches between crib slats, no corner posts over ¹⁄₁₆ inch high, and no cutouts in the headboard or footboard.

Baby Stock-Up Essentials

Optional Equipment

From a bathtub to a baby monitor, list all of the optional equipment you'd like to receive or purchase for your baby. As you receive gifts or shop, check off which items you've acquired.

- ☐ _____
- ☐ _____
- ☐ _____
- ☐ _____
- ☐ _____
- ☐ _____
- ☐ _____
- ☐ _____
- ☐ _____
- ☐ _____
- ☐ _____
- ☐ _____
- ☐ _____
- ☐ _____
- ☐ _____
- ☐ _____
- ☐ _____
- ☐ _____
- ☐ _____
- ☐ _____
- ☐ _____

Baby Stock-Up Essentials

Clothes and Linens

When shopping for clothes and linens for your baby, stock up on the following essentials first, before buying designer gear that your baby may outgrow after using only once or twice. Also make sure that all sleepwear is fire-retardant.

Note: Don't make the mistake of assuming you need doubles of everything if you happen to be carrying twins. You can probably get away with having one-and-a-half times as much clothing as what you would need if you were only having a single baby.

- ❏ 2 hooded towel-and-washcloth sets
- ❏ 3 sets of fitted crib sheets
- ❏ 3 blankets
- ❏ Waterproof mattress pad featuring cloth on one side and plastic or rubber backing on the other side
- ❏ 12 extra-large receiving blankets
- ❏ 3 pairs of socks
- ❏ 3 sweaters (depending on the season)
- ❏ 2 cotton hats
- ❏ 1 snowsuit or bunting bag (depending on the season)
- ❏ 4 large bibs (necessary only if you're planning to formula-feed or if your baby spits up a lot)
- ❏ 2 dozen sleepers; 3 sleepers size 0–3 months; 9 sleepers size 3–6 months; 6 sleepers size 6–9 months; and 6 sleepers size 6–12 months. (This quantity assumes you will be doing laundry daily or every other day. If you don't do laundry that often, load up on some additional sleepers.)

 If someone makes you a quilt for your baby's crib, hang it on your baby's wall or make a point of using it on your baby's bed only while your baby is out of the crib. According to the American Academy of Pediatrics, pillows, quilts, comforters, sheepskins, and stuffed toys should not be used in a baby's bed. Keep your baby warm by dressing him in a sleeper, instead.

Baby Stock-Up Essentials

Breastfeeding Supplies

Whether you're planning to breastfeed exclusively or do so in combination with bottle-feeding, you'll need to express breast milk from time to time. Be sure you have the following on hand:

❏ Breast pump (handy even if you're not planning to spend much time away from your baby; it relieves engorgement during the early days and allows you to stockpile breast milk in the freezer)

❏ One or two nursing bras (you'll need more, but hold off on purchasing them until you can judge the size of your postpartum bosom)

❏ Four 4-ounce and two 8-ounce bottles for expressed breast milk

❏ Sterile milk storage bags (an alternative to pumping into bottles)

❏ Nipples (one of several brands, so that you can test which works best for your baby)

❏ Bottle brush and nipple brush

❏ Dishwasher basket or drying rack especially for bottles and nipples

❏ Bottle warmer to heat frozen breast milk

Bottle-Feeding Supplies

If you decide to bottle-feed your baby, either exclusively or in combination with breastfeeding, you'll need to purchase the following supplies:

❏ Six 8-ounce bottles and six 4-ounce bottles

❏ Disposable bottle liners (if you choose a bottle that needs them)

❏ Nipples (one each of several different brands to test which works the best)

❏ Six to twelve bottle covers or caps

❏ Liquid measuring cup (if you're using powdered formula)

❏ Infant formulas (a few each of several different brands to test)

❏ Dishwasher basket or drying rack especially for bottles and nipples

❏ Bottle warmer

Baby Stock-Up Essentials

Other Bits and Pieces

In addition to shopping for baby equipment and baby clothes, you'll also need to hit the baby department and the drugstore for other bits and pieces. Here's a list of items that you'll want to have on hand when your baby arrives.

- ❑ Acetaminophen (infant drops)
- ❑ Antibacterial ointment
- ❑ Antiseptic for cord care (if your caregiver recommends it)
- ❑ Baby brush and comb
- ❑ Baby nail scissors or clippers
- ❑ Baby shampoo
- ❑ Baby soap
- ❑ Baby wipes (cloth or disposable types)
- ❑ Calibrated medicine dropper, syringe, or medicine spoon
- ❑ Cotton balls and swabs
- ❑ Diaper bag
- ❑ Diaper cream
- ❑ Diaper pail with childproof latch; disposable liners
- ❑ 3 dozen cloth diapers; more if you're using a diaper service
- ❑ 3 diaper wraps (for cloth diapers) in newborn, small, and medium sizes
- ❑ 2 packages disposable diapers in newborn (don't overbuy; your baby may be allergic to a particular brand of diaper)
- ❑ 2 packages disposable diapers in the smallest size
- ❑ Mild detergent for washing baby clothes
- ❑ Nasal aspirator (bulb syringe)
- ❑ Petroleum jelly
- ❑ Soft washcloths
- ❑ Thermometer (rectal or regular)

Baby Stock-Up Essentials

Postpartum Essentials for Mom

While you're busy shopping for baby, don't forget to stock up on postpartum essentials for yourself.

❏ **The Mother of All sanitary napkins:** You'll need at least two large boxes of the most absorbent sanitary napkins (not tampons) you can find — ideally ones designed specifically for postpartum use.

❏ **Breast pads:** Washable cotton breast pads are not only the most economical and the most environmentally friendly, they're also more comfortable than paper breast pads.

❏ **Lanolin:** Lanolin soothes sore nipples.

❏ **A sports bottle and a Thermos:** You'll be unbelievably thirsty if you're breastfeeding, so always tote water or a decaf beverage.

❏ **Hemorrhoid care:** If you're blessed with this delightful byproduct of both pregnancy and the pushing stage of labor, keep the following items in your postpartum kit: premoistened hemorrhoid wipes, a bottle of witch hazel and some cotton balls, and a hemorrhoid cushion (a doughnut-shaped pillow)

 When you're putting together your layette and decorating the nursery, don't forget to take into account what the weather is likely to be when your baby arrives. You're probably shopping for baby gear a season or two before you actually need it and you don't want to end up falling in love with items of clothing you'll never see on your little one.

Diaper Bag Essentials

It's easy to overpack or underpack the first time you try to go anywhere with your new baby. Although you'll fine-tune the contents of your diaper bag as you get used to being on the go, use the following list to make sure you don't forget anything on your first outings. To save yourself some time, keep your diaper bag stocked with all of the non-perishable essentials, so that you have to grab only the perishables on your way out.

❑ A full day's supply of diapers (at least six to eight diapers while baby's a newborn — more if you're staying overnight)

❑ A travel-size package of baby wipes (for smaller messes, you can save money by carrying a series of damp washcloths in a resealable plastic bag)

❑ Several extra plastic shopping and resealable bags for bringing home soiled articles of clothing (both baby's and yours) or soiled cloth diapers

❑ A couple of rags, towels, or spare cloth diapers for wiping up spills and burping the baby

❑ One or two receiving blankets

❑ A change or two of clothing for baby

❑ A spare shirt for you

❑ Diaper rash ointment

❑ A couple of toys

❑ A camera

❑ If your baby is breastfed and going to be away from you for part of the day: a bottle or two of expressed breast milk and an ice pack to keep it cool.

❑ If bottle-feeding: formula, one or two bottles, and a bib or two

❑ Snack(s) for you

❑ Bottle of water for you

Pediatrician Checklist

If you intend to have your baby cared for by your regular family doctor, your job is already done. But if you're hoping to have your baby seen by a pediatrician, you should plan to start looking for Dr. Right long before your baby is born. When you're interviewing prospective pediatricians (assuming, of course, that you actually have the luxury of being able to choose your baby's doctor), you'll want to ask the following questions:

How soon after the birth will the doctor see your baby? _____

_____

_____

When should your baby's subsequent checkups be scheduled? _____

_____

_____

What are the doctor's office hours? Are evening, early morning, or week-end appointments available? _____

_____

_____

Are certain days and times set aside for various types of visits such as well-baby checkups, immunizations, or special consultations? _____

_____

_____

Does the doctor or someone on his staff reply to phone calls during the day from patients and, if so, how long it typically takes to get a call back?

_____

_____

Does the doctor take emergency calls after hours, and if not, who does?

_____

_____

Who covers the practice when the doctor is unavailable? _____

_____

Baby-Proofing 101

Despite what you think, decorating the nursery doesn't have to be an exercise in endurance. In fact, the simpler you keep your nursery preparations, the more likely you are to decorate a room that's safe for your baby and can grow with your child. When shopping for furniture, decorating items, and safety supplies, be sure to stock up on the following:

❑ Bottom-heavy furniture or furniture you can attach to walls

❑ Scrubbable vinyl wallpaper or wallpaper border

❑ Hardwood flooring or stain-resistant carpeting with flecks of color

❑ Satin-finish, washable paint in mid tones

❑ Flame-retardant fabric for curtains

❑ Roller blinds (no blinds or curtains with cords)

❑ Baby-friendly plants (call your local poison control center for details)

❑ Wall-mounted baby gates for the top (and, if necessary, the bottom) of each set of stairs

❑ Screen guards (safety devices that are designed to catch the screen and your baby if your baby starts to fall out the window)

❑ Door alarms for all exterior doors

❑ Fire extinguishers for each exit to your home

❑ New batteries for your smoke detector(s)

❑ Plastic safety covers and cord locks for electrical outlets

❑ Corner guards for sharp-edged tables

❑ Baby-proof latches on drawers and cupboard doors

❑ Childproof latch for the toilet seat

❑ Bath mats for each bathtub

❑ A lockable cash box or medium-sized fishing-tackle box for all medications and vitamins

Baby-Proofing 101

❑ A safe toy box with a safety hinge to prevent the lid from closing too quickly and ventilation holes to ensure that your baby will be able to breathe if he happens to get trapped inside.

Baby Toys

Be sure to invest only in toys that will be safe for your baby to play with or be around. These include:

❑ Age-appropriate toys (you can download a PDF document containing the American Academy of Pediatrics' guidelines for age-appropriate toys for children from www.ihc.com/xp/ihc/documents/pcmc/toysafety.pdf)

❑ Flame-retardant plush toys (Note: For safety reasons, plush toys should never be put into a crib.)

❑ Toys that aren't so large they could suffocate a baby while playing

❑ Battery compartments that can be opened only with a screwdriver

❑ Toys that haven't been subject to any recalls (you can find out what toys have been subject to recalls by visiting the U.S. Consumer Product Safety Commission Web site at www.cpsc.gov or the Health Canada Web site at www.hc-sc.ga.ca)

❑ Mobiles that hang well above the crib (you don't want your baby to be able to pull the mobile down, scaring or injuring himself)

Steer clear of:

❑ Toys that have small parts, buttons, and other items that may come loose and pose a choking hazard

❑ Toys that have drawstrings or other dangling strings that may pose a strangulation risk

Gift Registries

To avoid ending up with six strollers and three high chairs, you'll want to keep track of the stores where you and your baby are registered. One advantage of living in the Information Age is that you may be able to check your gift registry online, figuring out which items you'll be receiving and which ones you may still need to purchase. Before registering with any store, be sure the store's return policy allows you to return items. Also, some stores offer discounts just before your due date in an effort to encourage you to purchase some of the remaining items on your list (yep, the big corporations have figured how to tap into that hormone-driven pre-baby nesting instinct!).

Store: _____
Web Address: _____
Username/Password: _____
Discounts: _____
Return Policy: _____
Notes: _____
_____

Store: _____
Web Address: _____
Username/Password: _____
Discounts: _____
Return Policy: _____
Notes: _____
_____

Store: _____
Web Address: _____
Username/Password: _____
Discounts: _____
Return Policy: _____
Notes: _____
_____

Baby Shower Gifts and Thank You's

While there's nothing wrong with simply heading over to the card store and picking up a package of thank-you cards, some parents-to-be prefer to get creative with their thank you's. Here are a few ideas you may want to try:

✎ Design a thank-you card on your computer. You can print out post-cards or traditional note cards using the stationery products available in most office supply stores.

✎ Use rubber stamps and blank note cards to design an eye-catching thank-you note. (You may look for some rubber stamps that tie into the baby theme — perhaps diaper pins or baby footprints.)

✎ Tie a thank-you tag around the neck of a miniature teddy bear or rubber duck.

✎ Use your digital camera to take a photo of your baby using the baby gift and then incorporate the image in your own e-greeting card.

Finding time to write thank-you notes for all the baby gifts that are likely to come your way can be a bit overwhelming when you're getting by on next-to-no sleep. That's why it's a good idea to write as many of your thank you notes as you can before your baby arrives. (Fortunately, a lot of your baby gifts will show up before your baby, so it's possible to get a bit of a head start on thank you's.)

Baby Shower Gifts and Thank You's

Gift Description	Given By	Date Received	Thank You Sent?

Baby Shower Gifts and Thank You's

Gift Description	Given By	Date Received	Thank You Sent?

Baby Shower Gifts and Thank You's

Gift Description	Given By	Date Received	Thank You Sent?

Baby Shower Gifts and Thank You's

Gift Description	Given By	Date Received	Thank You Sent?

What's in a Name?

Choosing a name for your baby is likely to be one of the tougher decisions you'll have to make during the next nine-and-a-half months. With thousands of names to choose from and your baby's sex a possible wild card, you could find yourself playing endless rounds of the baby name game.

You can use these pages to come up with a shortlist of names and — with any luck — you'll manage to zero in on the perfect name — or names — long before little Matthew or Emily decides to make his or her grand entrance. Keep a running list of the names under consideration and use the notes space to jot down any important details you'd like to remember about the name: its origin, its meaning, who suggested it, any alternative spellings, what place it may hold in your family's history, and so on.

You probably know of at least a few unfortunate souls whose sleep-deprived parents were clearly on autopilot when choosing a baby name — you know, the Quinten Egberts of the world! To save your own offspring from suffering the same sorry fate, you'll want to keep these important rules in mind when you're choosing a name for Junior:

- Steer clear of names that are overly pretentious or that are so trendy that they're doomed to sound dated by the time your child starts preschool.
- Look for a name that will grow with your child. Remember, what's cute for a baby may look downright silly on a business card.
- Stick with names that work well with your last name. Consider first name and last name combos that clash and look at whether your child's initials will spell any obscenities. (Hey, it happens.)
- If you decide to name your child after someone who is special to you, make sure that person is likely to remain within your circle of nearest and dearest for years to come — and stay out of prison, to boot.
- Keep the spelling simple. Your child will thank you for it, and so will all her teachers.
- Be prepared to go back to the drawing board if everyone else in your childbirth classes has picked the same name. (Do you really want your child to be one of a dozen Alicias in her kindergarten class?)

What's in a Name?

Name	Notes

What's in a Name?

Name	Notes

What's in a Name?

Name	Notes

Notes

Notes

Notes

Gearing Up for Delivery

Gearing Up for Delivery

This section is designed to help you keep track of the all the preparations you're making for the big day. Here, you'll find mini-address books to keep track of your pregnancy and labor support team, people who have volunteered to drive you to the hospital, friends and family who are ready to pitch in after the baby is born, and your postpartum doula or other service providers you may want to turn to for information and support after the birth.

You'll also find a handy place to keep track of your prenatal classes, plus checklists of people to call or e-mail when you're ready to announce your baby's arrival.

This section also includes lists of what to pack in your labor bag and suitcase, how to get things organized on the home front, and how to get your financial act together before the labor contractions start to kick in.

In short, this section gets you ready for the big day, so that when it comes, you can focus on your baby without having to worry about the rest of your life.

Getting to the Hospital

Keep a running list of people who are willing to act as chauffeur when the moment of truth arrives. (It goes without saying that you want to have more than one name on the list in case your chauffeur-designate is unavailable when your baby decides to make her grand entrance.)

Driver: _____

Home phone number: _____

Work phone number: _____

Cell phone number: _____

Name of backup driver: _____

Home phone number: _____

Work phone number: _____

Cell phone number: _____

Name of backup driver: _____

Home phone number: _____

Work phone number: _____

Cell phone number: _____

Taxi company: _____

Phone number: _____

If your driver isn't familiar with the route to the hospital, consider stapling directions or a map to this page. You don't want to play navigator in between labor contractions!

Prenatal Classes

Use these pages to track the date, time, and other details about the childbirth classes, breastfeeding classes, hospital tours and visits, and any other classes you choose to attend.

Class: _____

Date/Time: _____

Instructor: _____

Confirmation number: _____

Bring: _____
_____

Class: _____

Date/Time: _____

Instructor: _____

Confirmation number: _____

Bring: _____
_____

Class: _____

Date/Time: _____

Instructor: _____

Confirmation number: _____

Bring: _____
_____

Class: _____

Date/Time: _____

Instructor: _____

Confirmation number: _____

Bring: _____
_____

Prenatal Classes

Class: _____
Date/Time: _____
Instructor: _____
Confirmation number: _____
Bring: _____
_____

Class: _____
Date/Time: _____
Instructor: _____
Confirmation number: _____
Bring: _____
_____

Class: _____
Date/Time: _____
Instructor: _____
Confirmation number: _____
Bring: _____
_____

Class: _____
Date/Time: _____
Instructor: _____
Confirmation number: _____
Bring: _____
_____

Prenatal Classes

Class: _____
Date/Time: _____
Instructor: _____
Confirmation number: _____
Bring: _____
_____

Class: _____
Date/Time: _____
Instructor: _____
Confirmation number: _____
Bring: _____
_____

Class: _____
Date/Time: _____
Instructor: _____
Confirmation number: _____
Bring: _____
_____

Class: _____
Date/Time: _____
Instructor: _____
Confirmation number: _____
Bring: _____
_____

Getting Your Support Team in Place

Community and professional help is available to you after you deliver your baby. From 24-hour parent information lines to groups and clinics offering breastfeeding support, ask your caregiver about the following resources and note his or her responses here.

What services are available in your community, both through health care and family service agencies and nonprofit community groups like La Leche League (a group that offers support to breastfeeding mothers)?

_____

_____

_____

_____

Does your local hospital or health unit offer a 24-hour parent information phone line that is staffed by a maternal/infant nurse or other qualified health professional? _____

_____

_____

_____

Does your health unit offer a breastfeeding support network that matches up experienced nursing mothers with first-timers? _____

_____

_____

_____

Does your health unit or hospital provide home visits and/or telephone support from a public health nurse and/or a lactation consultant? _____

_____

_____

_____

Getting Your Support Team in Place

Keep a running list of the names and phone numbers of friends and family members who've offered to help so that you'll be able to call in any and all favors after the baby arrives. Chores to delegate include cooking, dishwashing, laundry folding, dusting, vacuuming, caring for other kids, and so on.

Name	Phone Number	Availability	Potential Tasks

Countdown to Motherhood

Stocking Up and Planning Ahead

Use the weeks leading up to your baby's grand entrance to do whatever you can to make your life easier when the baby arrives:

- Stock your home with healthy foods that can be eaten with one hand.
- Fill your freezer with a variety of precooked entrées.
- Stay on top of the laundry during your final weeks of pregnancy.
- Keep the kitchen and bathroom reasonably clean.
- Set up baby change stations on each floor of your house.
- Reorganize your kitchen cupboards so that the items you need most often are all within easy reach.
- Prepay as many bills as possible.
- Reevaluate your life insurance needs.
- Write a will.
- Pick up cards and gifts for any upcoming birthdays or anniversaries.
- Get a head start on your baby announcements. (Hint: You can pre-address and stamp the envelopes and fill out some of the information on the actual announcements.)
- Take care of as many routine appointments (eye appointments, haircuts) as possible now.
- Plan your "babymoon" — time alone as a family during your baby's first few days of life — with your partner.

 For more information on planning your "babymoon," go to www.pregnancylibrary.com. You'll find suggestions on making the transition to parenthood as stress free as possible for you and your partner.

Countdown to Motherhood

The Last Hurrah

At some point during the next few weeks, you will finally get to meet your new baby. That means this is your last chance to take advantage of the perks of the pre-baby lifestyle — in other words, your last hurrah! Here are ten experiences you'll definitely want to squeeze in before baby makes his or her grand entrance.

- Spontaneous sex
- Time alone with your partner
- A meal at a fancy restaurant
- A night at the movies
- An evening out with your girlfriends
- The spiciest meal your pregnant body can handle
- The chance to play Demi Moore by posing for a few pregnancy portraits (it's up to you whether you opt to go for the fully clothed look or something a little more *au naturel*!)
- The chance to sleep in
- A nice, warm bubble bath
- The opportunity to write one final pre-baby love letter to your partner (your chance to reassure your partner that while things may be a little crazy during the weeks ahead, you're looking forward to embarking on this adventure called parenthood together)

People to Call

Your friends and family want to know your baby's sex, name, height, and weight the moment she's born. On these two pages, jot down the names and phone numbers of close friends and relatives who need to know right away. For other friends, coworkers, and more-distant relatives, create a group e-mail address before the birth so that you can fire off a single e-mail message and send it to the entire gang at once. (Hint: If you hold off on announcing your news to your "B-list" friends for a day or two, you'll limit the number of congratulatory phone calls that come your way while you're trying to catch up on the sleep you missed out on while you were in labor. The moment you hit the Send button, your phone is going to start ringing off the hook.)

Name	Phone Number(s)	E-mail Address

People to Call

Name	Phone Number(s)	E-mail Address

Packing Your Bags

Wondering what types of items your labor bag should contain? The following items are pretty much de rigueur if you're planning to give birth in a hospital or at a birth center.

❑ Your health insurance card and pre-registration forms

❑ One or more copies of your birth plan

❑ Sponges (to help keep you cool)

❑ A tennis ball or rolling pin (ideally one that can be filled with hot or cold water) to massage your back

❑ A frozen freezer pack (small) wrapped in a hand towel

❑ A picture or other object that you find comforting (for positive visualization during labor)

❑ Massage oil or lotion

❑ Cornstarch or other non-perfumed powder to reduce friction during massage

❑ A hot water bottle

❑ Lip balm or petroleum jelly to relieve dry lips

❑ A camera or video camera plus spare batteries and spare film

❑ Extra pillows in colored pillow cases (so your pillows and pillow cases don't get mixed up with the hospital's or birth center's)

❑ A portable stereo and some cassette tapes or CDs

❑ Paper and pens

❑ A roll of quarters, a prepaid phone card, or a cell phone

❑ Snacks and drinks for your partner

❑ A bathing suit for your partner (so that he can accompany you in the shower or the Jacuzzi to help you to work through contractions)

❑ A change of clothes for your partner (in case your labor ends up being very long)

❑ Books, magazines, a deck of cards, and other ways to pass the time

Packing Your Bags

You'll want to pack the following items in your suitcase for after you deliver:

- ❏ Hairbrush
- ❏ Shampoo
- ❏ Soap
- ❏ Toothbrush
- ❏ Toothpaste
- ❏ Deodorant
- ❏ Highly absorbent sanitary pads
- ❏ Birth announcements and a pen
- ❏ Earplugs
- ❏ A small gift for each of the baby's siblings (unless, of course, this is baby number one!)
- ❏ Two or more nightgowns, front-opening style
- ❏ A bathrobe
- ❏ Two or more nursing bras
- ❏ Five or more pair of disposable or inexpensive underwear (they may get badly stained from the heavy post-delivery bleeding)
- ❏ Two pairs of warm socks
- ❏ A pair of slippers
- ❏ A going-home outfit for you (something that fit when you were five or six months pregnant)
- ❏ A going-home outfit for the baby (ideally a sleeper plus a hat)
- ❏ A receiving blanket
- ❏ A bunting bag and/or a heavy blanket if it's wintertime
- ❏ A diaper for your baby to wear home (just in case the hospital uses cloth diapers)

Service Providers to Call

In addition to friends and family, various service providers also need to be notified of your baby's birth.

Name	Phone Number	Account Number
Health insurance company		
Life insurance agent		
Financial planner		
Pediatrician		
Postpartum doula		
Diaper service		
Cleaning service		
Daycare center		
Lawyer (if applicable)		
Clergy (if applicable)		

Notes

Notes

Baby's Grand Entrance

Baby's Grand Entrance

This section is designed to be put to use as you head into the home stretch of your pregnancy. Consequently, it's packed with all the need-to-know information about preparing for baby's grand entrance: how to tell when you're *really* in labor, when to call your doctor or midwife, and when to head to the hospital.

Because your baby doesn't come with an "owner's manual," this section also offers plenty of space to write down take-home instructions for caring for your new baby, as well as the healthcare team's advice on breastfeeding and caring for your postpartum body.

After you're settled in at home, your child's well-baby visits to her pediatrician or your family doctor begin. How often your baby goes in for a checkup depends on your doctor's preferences, but babies are often seen at two to four days, two weeks, one month, and two months, with additional visits every few months after that. This section provides you with opportunities to record the results of those visits. (Note: If you're being cared for by a midwife, your baby may be seen by your midwife initially before responsibility for your baby's care is transferred to the pediatrician or family doctor. You can record the results of those initial midwife visits here, too.)

If you delivered vaginally and had an uncomplicated pregnancy, your doctor will probably schedule an appointment for you somewhere between four to eight weeks after you deliver your baby. You'll want to use this section of the planner to keep track of your post-delivery questions for your caregiver and to note any tips or recommendations coming out of your postpartum checkup.

How to Tell Whether You're in Labor

If you experience the following symptoms, chances are you're experiencing a powerful dress rehearsal for the main event rather than true labor.

- Your contractions are irregular and are increasing neither in frequency nor severity.

- Your contractions subside if you rest, change position, or have two large glasses of water.

- The pain is centered in your lower abdomen rather than in your lower back.

- Your bloody show is brownish-tinged rather than red-tinged and likely the result of either an internal examination or intercourse within the previous 48 hours.

Assume it's the real thing rather than a convincing imitation if you experience the following symptoms:

- Your contractions are getting longer, stronger, more painful, and more frequent, and they're falling into some sort of regular pattern.

- Your contractions intensify if you move around and aren't relieved by either a change of position or by consuming two large glasses of water.

- The pain is radiating from your lower back and spreading to your lower abdomen and possibly your legs, as well.

- You feel as though you're experiencing a gastrointestinal upset and you are having some diarrhea.

- You're passing blood-streaked or pinkish mucus (bloody show).

- Your membranes have ruptured.

How to Tell Whether You're In Labor

The following chart can help you to track the interval (the length of time between the start of each contraction) and the duration (the length) of your contractions. If you make a point of noting the start time and the end time of each contraction and calculating the interval and frequency of each contraction, you will be able to let your caregiver know how long your contractions are lasting, how frequently they are occurring, and whether they are falling into any predictable pattern. This is important information for your doctor or midwife to have when he or she is trying to assess how your labor is progressing.

Count	Start Time	End Time	Duration	Interval/ Frequency
1				
2				
3				
4				
5				
6				
7				
8				
9				
10				
11				
12				
13				
14				
15				
16				
17				
18				
19				
20				
21				

How to Tell Whether You're In Labor

Count	Start Time	End Time	Duration	Interval/ Frequency
22				
23				
24				
25				
26				
27				
28				
29				
30				
31				
32				
33				
34				
35				
36				
37				
38				
39				
40				
41				
42				
43				
44				
45				
46				
47				
48				
49				
50				
51				

How to Tell Whether You're In Labor

Count	Start Time	End Time	Duration	Interval/ Frequency
52				
53				
54				
55				
56				
57				
58				
59				
60				
61				
62				
63				
64				
65				
66				
67				
68				
69				
70				
71				
72				
73				
74				
75				
76				
77				
78				
79				
80				
81				

When Contractions Start

Call your caregiver as soon as you experience any of the following symptoms. Plan to make this phone call yourself; your caregiver will be able to get a good sense of how far along your labor is simply by listening to your voice.

- Your contractions are strong and regular (generally at five-minute intervals, unless your caregiver asks you to call sooner than this).

- Your membranes have ruptured or you suspect they've ruptured.

- You experience a lot of bleeding (which can indicate premature separation of the placenta or a blockage of the cervical opening).

- You notice thickish green fluid coming from your vagina (which can indicate that your baby has passed meconium into the amniotic fluid).

- There's a loop of umbilical cord dangling from your vagina or you feel something inside your vagina (a possible indication of a cord prolapse). If you suspect you've experienced a cord prolapse, lie with your head and chest on the floor and your bottom in the air and have someone call an ambulance. This will help to prevent your baby's head from compressing the umbilical cord and interrupting the flow of oxygen.

In general, plan to head to the hospital when the following occurs:

- Your contractions are four minutes apart, lasting one minute and occurring consistently for one hour or more.

- Your contractions are so painful that you have to rely on your relaxation breathing or other pain-management techniques.

- You can no longer talk during a contraction.

- You instinctively feel that it's time to go.

Of course, if you live a significant distance from the hospital, you're giving birth in the middle of a snowstorm, or you have a history of rapid labors, you'll want to hit the road sooner rather than later.

Meeting Your Baby

Within one minute of your baby's birth, he is given an APGAR test to see how he's faring and to determine whether he needs additional attention. After that, your newborn is carefully examined by his team of caregivers throughout his first day of life. Use this space to record the results of your baby's first tests:

Height: _____

Weight: _____

Blood Pressure: _____

Body temperature: _____

Blood Type: _____

Other test results, procedures performed, or notes: _____

_____

_____

_____

_____

The Moment You Met

Record details of the first time you and your baby met face to face:

_____

_____

_____

_____

_____

_____

Take-Home Care Instructions

Need a baby "owner's manual"? Use the advice of professionals and the other knowledgeable people around you to create your own baby operating instructions.

Umbilical cord care: _____

_____

_____

Bathing: _____

_____

_____

Feeding: _____

_____

_____

Sleep concerns: _____

_____

_____

Crying/colic: _____

_____

_____

Other advice: _____

_____

_____

_____

_____

_____

_____

Take-Home Care Instructions

How to Tell Whether Your Baby Is Sick

Your baby will get sick from time to time, in spite of your best efforts. You can expect your baby to experience one or more of the following symptoms if he's doing battle with an illness:

- **Behavioral changes:** Your baby becomes uncharacteristically fussy and irritable or sleepy and lethargic.

- **Change in skin color:** Your baby suddenly becomes pale or flushed; or the whites of his eyes take on a yellowish or pinkish hue.

- **Coughing:** Your baby starts coughing because there is some sort of irritation in the respiratory tract — anywhere from the nose to the lungs.

- **Croup:** Your baby's breathing becomes very noisy (some babies become very hoarse and develop a cough that sounds like a seal's bark) and, in severe cases, his windpipe may actually become obstructed.

- **Dehydration:** Your baby has a dry mouth, isn't drinking as much as usual, is urinating less often than usual, and doesn't shed tears when he cries. He may also be experiencing vomiting and/or diarrhea.

- **Diarrhea:** Your baby's bowel movements become more frequent, become watery, or are unformed. Diarrhea is often accompanied by abdominal cramps or a stomachache.

- **Fever:** Your baby's temperature is higher than normal — something that often indicates the presence of an infection but that can also be caused by a reaction to an immunization or overdressing your baby.

- **Rashes:** Your baby develops some sort of skin rash.

- **Runny nose:** Your baby's nose starts secreting clear, colorless mucus that may become thick and yellowish or greenish within a day or two.

- **Vomiting:** Your baby begins vomiting often enough to become dehydrated or your child chokes and inhales vomit.

- **Wheezing:** Your baby makes wheezing sounds that are particularly noticeable when he's breathing out.

Take-Home Care Instructions

When to Call the Pediatrician

You don't want to jump the gun and call your pediatrician every time your baby has the sniffles, but do call in the following circumstances:

- Your baby's temperature (taken by rectal thermometer) is too high for a child his age: 100.2°F for zero to two months; 101°F for three to six months; 103°F for six months or older. If you opt to use an axillary thermometer (one that takes the baby's temperature under the arm), this reading tends to be about a degree-and-a-half lower.

- Your baby has had a fever for a couple of days.

- He is crying or whimpering inconsolably or seems cranky or irritable.

- He's having difficulty waking up or seems listless and confused.

- He's limp or weak.

- He's having convulsions (if he turned blue during the seizure, had convulsions that lasted more than a few minutes, had difficulty breathing after the seizure passed, or still seems drowsy or lethargic an hour later, seek emergency medical assistance).

- The soft spot (fontanel) on his head is beginning to swell or recede.

- He appears to have a stiff neck, headache, or stomach pain.

- He has purple (not red) spots on the skin or large purple blotches (possible signs of meningitis, an infection of the brain).

- He has developed a skin rash or is noticeably flushed or pale.

- He's having difficulty breathing (a possible sign of asthma or pneumonia).

- He is refusing to drink or nurse.

- He has constant vomiting or diarrhea.

- He is unable to swallow and is drooling excessively (a possible sign of epiglottitis, a life-threatening infection that causes swelling in the back of the throat).

- You know that he has a weakened immune system as the result of a preexisting medical condition.

Feeding Advice

If you're new to the world of breastfeeding, you may find yourself with a lot of questions about the art and science of nursing a baby. You can jot down your questions and your caregiver's answers here. This is also a great place to note any breastfeeding advice you receive from nurses, lactation consultants, and other breastfeeding experts.

If you're bottle-feeding your baby, you need to get acquainted with bottle-feeding equipment, types of formula available, amount to feed, and when to feed your baby. Use this space to keep track of the advice your caregiver offers about bottle-feeding your baby.

_____

_____

_____

_____

_____

_____

_____

_____

_____

_____

_____

_____

_____

_____

_____

Feeding Advice

Advice for Your Postpartum Care

Jot down instructions on your postpartum care that you receive from your caregiver and maternity nurse. Here are a few of the key questions you may want to ask before leaving the hospital:

What are your recommendations regarding caring for the perineal area during the postpartum period? _____

_____

Do I need to do anything special to care for my episiotomy site and/or hemorrhoids? _____

_____

What do I need to know about recovering from a cesarean section?

_____

_____

Do you have any tips on coping with breast engorgement or nipple soreness? Whom should I call if I have breastfeeding questions or concerns?

_____

_____

When can I start exercising again? What types of exercise are recommended during the postpartum period? Are there any exercise restrictions I need to keep in mind? _____

_____

At what point am I likely to start feeling like having sex again? How will I know when my body has recovered enough from the birth for me to start having intercourse again? _____

_____

When should I start using birth control? Should I go back to using the birth control method I was using before I had my baby or should I consider switching to another birth control method? _____

_____

_____

Advice for Your Postpartum Care

Well-Baby Visit 1

Q&A
Questions to ask your baby's doctor:

Well-Baby Visit 1

Stats and Exam Results

Record the stats and test results from this visit to your baby's doctor.

Date and time of visit: _____

Height: _____

Weight: _____

Other measurements: _____

Temperature: _____

Reflexes: _____

Immunizations: _____

_____

_____

Developmental milestones: _____

_____

_____

Going Forward

Answers, advice, and other notes from your visit:

_____

_____

_____

_____

_____

_____

_____

_____

Well-Baby Visit 2

Q&A
Questions to ask your baby's doctor:

_____

_____

_____

_____

_____

_____

_____

_____

_____

_____

_____

_____

_____

_____

_____

_____

_____

_____

_____

_____

_____

Well-Baby Visit 2

Stats and Exam Results

Record the stats and test results from this visit to your baby's doctor.

Date and time of visit: _____

Height: _____

Weight: _____

Other measurements: _____

Temperature: _____

Reflexes: _____

Immunizations: _____

_____

_____

Developmental milestones: _____

_____

_____

Going Forward

Answers, advice, and other notes from your visit:

_____

_____

_____

_____

_____

_____

_____

_____

Well-Baby Visit 3

Q&A
Questions to ask your baby's doctor:

Well-Baby Visit 3

Stats and Exam Results

Record the stats and test results from this visit to your baby's doctor.

Date and time of visit: _____

Height: _____

Weight: _____

Other measurements: _____

Temperature: _____

Reflexes: _____

Immunizations: _____

_____

_____

Developmental milestones: _____

_____

_____

Going Forward

Answers, advice, and other notes from your visit:

_____

_____

_____

_____

_____

_____

_____

_____

_____

Well-Baby Visit 4

Q&A
Questions to ask your baby's doctor:

_____

_____

_____

_____

_____

_____

_____

_____

_____

_____

_____

_____

_____

_____

_____

_____

_____

_____

_____

_____

_____

_____

_____

Well-Baby Visit 4

Stats and Exam Results

Record the stats and test results from this visit to your baby's doctor.

Date and time of visit: _____

Height: _____

Weight: _____

Other measurements: _____

Temperature: _____

Reflexes: _____

Immunizations: _____

_____

_____

Developmental milestones: _____

_____

_____

Going Forward

Answers, advice, and other notes from your visit:

_____

_____

_____

_____

_____

_____

_____

_____

Your Postpartum Checkup

Q&A
Questions to ask your doctor or midwife:

_____

_____

_____

_____

_____

_____

_____

_____

_____

_____

_____

_____

_____

_____

_____

_____

_____

_____

_____

_____

_____

_____

_____

Your Postpartum Checkup

Stats and Exam Results
Record the stats and test results from your postpartum visit.

Date and time of visit: _____

Weight: _____

Blood pressure: _____

Pulse: _____

Urinalysis results: _____

Pap/pelvic results: _____

Other test results: _____

_____

_____

Going Forward
Recommendations and advice from your caregiver:

_____

_____

_____

_____

_____

_____

_____

_____

_____

_____

_____

Birth Announcements Organizer

Looking to do something a little out of the ordinary with your baby announcements (assuming, of course, that you have the time and the energy to do anything more than sticking stamps on preprinted announcements)? Here are a few ideas:

❏ Design a birth announcement on your computer, print it on iron-on paper, and iron it on to a baby bib, onesie, or infant-sized T-shirt.

❏ Using a fabric pen, write your baby's vital statistics (for example, date of birth, weight, length) on a onesie or a T-shirt. Take a photo of your baby wearing the shirt and incorporate the photo into your birth announcement.

❏ Take one photo of your megapregnant belly (either fully clothed or au naturel) and one of your newborn baby. Use them as before-and-after shots in your birth announcement.

❏ Send everyone on your birth announcement list a page from your baby's scrapbook, along with a self-addressed, stamped envelope. Ask each person to do something special with the page: write a letter to your baby, share a recipe or a poem, share words of wisdom or a story, or find some other memorable way of welcoming your baby.

Of course, if you're more into the low-maintenance baby announcement regime (and last time I checked, that wasn't a crime!), you may want to think about doing the following:

❏ Preaddress your baby announcements and fill out as much information as possible ahead of time; for example, your name, your partner's name, and so on.

❏ Design your baby announcements on your computer so that you can simply fill in the vital statistics at the last minute and hit the Print button.

❏ Send out an e-mail announcement or electronic greeting card so that you don't have to spend time addressing envelopes or sticking on stamps.

❏ Announce your baby's birth at a baby announcement Web site and direct friends and relatives to an online photo album.

Birth Announcements Organizer

Use this space to fill in the names and addresses of everyone you'd like to receive a birth announcement. Just fill in the names and addresses as in the example below.

Jane Smith 100 Center Way City, State 10000		

Birth Announcements Organizer

Birth Announcements Organizer

Birth Announcements Organizer

Birth Announcements Organizer

Baby Gifts and Thank You's

After your baby is born, you'll likely receive a few more gifts. (Some people consider a tiny wrapped parcel to be the price of admission to sneak a peek at the new arrival!) Keep track of your baby gifts and your thank you notes here so you can be sure everyone was properly thanked.

Gift Description	Given By	Date Received	Thank You Sent?

Baby Gifts and Thank You's

Gift Description	Given By	Date Received	Thank You Sent?

Baby Gifts and Thank You's

Gift Description	Given By	Date Received	Thank You Sent?

Baby Gifts and Thank You's

Gift Description	Given By	Date Received	Thank You Sent?

Baby Gifts and Thank You's

Gift Description	Given By	Date Received	Thank You Sent?

Baby Gifts and Thank You's

Gift Description	Given By	Date Received	Thank You Sent?

Notes

Notes

Resource Guide

Resource Guide

Because food is probably always on your mind (you're either craving your favorite foods, steering clear of those that trigger nausea, or worrying about those foods that are known to be harmful to your developing baby), this section is jam-packed with food facts that allow you to make the healthiest possible choices for you and your baby. As you make your way through this part of the planner, you'll definitely want to check out the lists of nutrient-rich foods, as well as foods that can increase and decrease nausea. And you'll want to read through the guide to "nutrition on the go" for busy moms (a great way to start thinking ahead about eating healthfully after your baby arrives).

And speaking of handy reference tools, check out the medications guide included in this section before taking any over-the-counter product. Many of the medications that you take on a regular basis may be off-limits to you while you're pregnant.

In this section, you also find lists of symptoms that require a call to your doctor or a visit to the hospital — those that may be cause for concern during and after pregnancy, such as the symptoms of premature labor and postpartum depression.

Finally, in this section, you'll find ten months' worth of calendar pages. Use them to keep track of all your appointments (pregnancy related or not) in one place so that you don't miss a beat over the next ten crazy — but fun — months of your life.

Food Taboos

When pregnant, you'll want to steer clear of these potentially dangerous foods:

* Hot dogs unless they are reheated until they are steaming hot

* Luncheon meats or deli meats (ham, salami, bologna) unless they are reheated until steaming hot

* Uncooked or undercooked meat, poultry, or fish (especially shellfish)

* Refrigerated smoked seafood (unless it's in a cooked entrée, such as a casserole); shelf-stable smoked seafood can be eaten

* King mackerel, shark, swordfish, and tilefish

* Excessive quantities of fish (The U.S. Food and Drug Administration recommends eating no more than 12 ounces per week of cooked fish, and recommends eating a variety of species.)

* Raw eggs and foods containing raw or partially cooked eggs

* Soft cheeses such as feta, brie, Camembert, blue-veined cheeses, and Mexican-style cheeses such as "queso blanco fresco." (It's still okay to eat hard cheeses; semisoft cheeses such as mozzarella; pasteurized processed cheeses such as slices and spreads; cream cheese; and cottage cheese.)

* Unpasteurized milk and foods that contain unpasteurized milk

* Refrigerated pâté or meat spreads; shelf-stable pâté and meat spreads can be eaten

* Unpasteurized juices

* Raw sprouts, especially alfalfa sprouts

* Herbal supplements and teas

🖊 Talk to your caregiver for specific recommendations regarding caffeine consumption. The March of Dimes recommends limiting caffeine to no more than two cups of coffee per day (or the equivalent amount of caffeine, less than 300 mg per day).

🖊 Alcohol (discuss specifics with your caregiver)

🖊 Other foods, as directed by your caregiver:

The experts don't always see eye to eye about which foods you should avoid during pregnancy. If you want to do some additional research on this topic, talk to your caregiver and check out the following excellent sources of information.

On food contamination and methylmercury consumption:

- Visit the March of Dimes at: www.marchofdimes.com/pnhec/159_826.asp

- Find the FDA's warnings on mercury contamination at: http://vm.cfsan.fda.gov/~dms/admehg.html

- Read the USDA's recommendations regarding listeriosis at: www.fsis.usda.gov/OA/pubs/lm_tearsheet.htm

- Review nutrition for a healthy pregnancy issued by Health Canada at: www.hc-sc.gc.ca/hpfb-dgpsa/onpp-bppn/national_guidelines_int_e.html

On caffeine:

- See the March of Dimes recommendations at: www.marchofdimes.com/pnhec/159_816.asp

- Get the Health Canada take at: www.hc-sc.gc.ca/hpfb-dgpsa/onpp-bppn/national_guidelines_int_e.html

Nutrient Cheat Sheet

You need certain nutrients to sustain a healthy pregnancy: calcium, vitamin D, folic acid, iron, and essential fatty acids. Use this cheat sheet to find foods that provide the nutrition you need.

What You Need	How Much You Need	Where to Find It	Why You Need It During Pregnancy
Calcium	1,200 to 1,500 mg per day (depending on age)	**Excellent sources** (275 mg/serving or more): milk, Swiss cheese, tofu set with calcium sulphate, plain yogurt, whole sesame seeds, fortified plant-based beverages **Good sources** (165 mg/serving or more): cheeses such as mozzarella, cheddar, Edam, brick, Parmesan, Gouda, processed cheese slices; and processed cheese spread; flavored yogurt; canned sardines, canned salmon (including bones) **Other foods containing calcium** (55 mg/serving or more): creamed cottage cheese, ricotta cheese, cooked or canned legumes (e.g., beans), cooked bok choy, kale, turnip greens, mustard greens, broccoli, oranges, cooked scallops, cooked oysters, almonds, dried sunflower seeds	To maintain your bones while providing for the development of your baby's skeletal system
Vitamin D	200 IU (international units)	**Excellent sources:** evaporated milk, fortified soy beverages, margarine, and fatty fish (e.g., salmon) **Good sources:** egg yolks	To increase the intestine's ability to absorb calcium and the body's ability to use it efficiently

Nutrient Cheat Sheet

What You Need	How Much You Need	Where to Find It	Why You Need It During Pregnancy
Folic acid	0.4 mg per day You'll have to make a conscious effort to add folic acid to your diet. A typical woman of childbearing age obtains just 0.2 mg per day from her diet. **Note:** Women with a higher-than-average risk of giving birth to a baby with a neural tube defect require 4.0 mg per day.	**Excellent sources** (more than 0.055 mg/serving): cooked fava, kidney, pinto, roman, soy, and white beans; chickpeas; lentils; cooked spinach; asparagus; romaine lettuce; orange juice; canned pineapple juice; sunflower seeds **Good sources** (more than 0.033 mg/serving): lima beans (cooked), corn, bean sprouts, broccoli (cooked), peas, Brussels sprouts, beets, green honeydew melons, raspberries, oranges, blackberries, avocado, roasted peanuts, wheat germ **Other foods containing folic acid** (0.011 mg or more): cooked carrots, beet greens, sweet potato, snow peas, summer or winter squash, rutabaga, cabbage, cooked green beans, cashews, roasted peanuts, walnuts, egg, strawberries, banana, grapefruit, cantaloupe, whole wheat or white bread, pork kidney, breakfast cereals, milk	To support your expanding blood volume, to promote the growth of both maternal and fetal tissues, and to decrease the risk of neural tube defects (NTDs)

Nutrient Cheat Sheet

What You Need	How Much You Need	Where to Find It	Why You Need It During Pregnancy
Iron	First trimester: 13 mg Second and third trimesters: 18 mg	**Excellent sources** (3.5 mg/serving or more): nonheme sources — cooked beans, white beans, soybeans, lentils, and chickpeas; clams and oysters; pumpkin, sesame, and squash seeds; iron-enriched breakfast cereals **Good sources** (2.1. mg/serving or more): heme sources — ground beef or steak, blood pudding. Non-heme sources — canned lima beans, red kidney beans, chickpeas, split peas, enriched cooked egg noodles, dried apricots **Other foods containing iron** (0.7 mg/serving or more): heme sources — chicken, ham, lamb, pork, veal, halibut, haddock, perch, salmon, shrimp, canned sardines, tuna, eggs. *Nonheme sources — peanuts, pecans, walnuts, pistachios, roasted almonds, roasted cashews, sunflower seeds, cooked egg noodles, bread, pumpernickel bagels, bran muffins, cooked oatmeal, wheat germ, canned beats (drained), canned pumpkin, raisins, peaches, prunes, apricots **	To increase the quantity of red blood cells and to supply the placenta and growing baby. Women who consume inadequate quantities of iron during pregnancy are at increased risk of experiencing premature delivery, giving birth to a low-birthweight baby, or experiencing fetal loss. They also tend to experience fatigue, reduced immunity to infection, and other problems.

Nutrient Cheat Sheet

What You Need	How Much You Need	Where to Find It	Why You Need It During Pregnancy
Essential fatty acids	Not applicable	Include sources of essential fatty acids such as soybean, and canola oils, and non-hydrogenated margarines; soy-based products (tofu, vegi burgers); and salad dressings made from nonhydrogenated oils such as canola or soybean oils in your diet. Limit your intake of fried foods, higher-fat commercial bakery products, and snack foods.	To promote proper fetal neural and visual development

* Note: Heme sources of iron (iron from meat, poultry, and fish) are more easily absorbed than nonheme sources. It's important not to pair foods containing nonheme types of iron with the following types of foods, all of which can interfere with iron absorption: tea, coffee, legumes, soybeans, whole grains, spinach, chard, beet greens, rhubarb, sweet potato, calcium.

** Note: An iron supplement (30 mg) is generally recommended during the second and third trimesters because many women will have depleted their pre-pregnancy iron stores by this point.

Foods That Increase/Decrease Nausea

Morning sickness is one of the most annoying pregnancy-related conditions, and it's definitely one of the most common, affecting between 60% and 80% of pregnant women. And while morning sickness does tend to be most severe in the morning, some women experience nausea and vomiting at other times of the day, too — which helps to explain why a growing number of health authorities are ditching the term "morning sickness" and choosing to go with the more medically accurate term "nausea and vomiting of pregnancy," instead. Here are some tips on coping with morning sickness:

- Don't overeat or get too hungry. Eat small, frequent meals and snack often.

- Don't drink fluids at mealtimes. Just make sure you make up for these lost fluids at other times of the day, because dehydration can also cause nausea!

- Eat something before you get out of bed and start moving around in the morning — you're less likely to get sideswiped by a wave of nausea.

- Identify your nausea triggers (foods and odors) and avoid them.

- Take your prenatal vitamin in the middle of a meal, instead of on an empty stomach.

- Choose stomach-friendly foods like yogurt and low-fat, high-carbohydrate foods, avoiding hard-to-digest foods like sausages, onion rings, and other fatty fried foods.

- Don't force yourself to eat foods that make you gag just because they're good for you. This is one time in your life when it's okay to turn your nose up at a serving of Brussels sprouts.

Foods That Increase/Decrease Nausea

Food Group	Stomach-Friendly Food Choices	Foods that Tend to Aggravate Morning Sickness
Grain products	Rice cakes, soda crackers, bagels, pasta, cereal, oatmeal	Spicy, high-fat crackers
Fruits and vegetables	Lemons (for sucking on or sniffing), bananas, applesauce, rhubarb, grapes, watermelon, pears, papaya juice, potatoes (baked, boiled, or mashed), avocados, celery sticks, carrot sticks, zucchini, tomatoes	Onions, cabbage, cauliflower
Milk products	Yogurt smoothies, frozen yogurt, puddings	High-fat cheeses
Meat and alternatives	Sunflower seeds	Fried meats, greasy foods, high-fat meats (sausages), fried eggs, spicy foods, foods containing monosodium glutamate (MSG)
Other foods	Ginger (root extract, fresh-ground, capsules, tea, sticks, crystals, pickled, and in other forms), mints (especially peppermint), lemon drops, licorice, potato chips, chewing gum, pickles, chamomile tea, lemonade, carbonated mineral water with a twist of lemon, sherbet	High-fat foods (e.g., french fries), fried foods (e.g., onion rings), spicy foods (e.g. corn chips), and beverages containing caffeine (e.g., coffee and cola)

Medications Guide

The active ingredients in most common over-the-counter medications are perfectly safe, but some can cause problems for you or your baby. Use this guide as a reference and check with your caregiver before taking any medication.

Active Ingredient	Possible Problems During Pregnancy
Acetaminophen (found in products such as Actifed Cold and Sinus; Alka-Seltzer Plus; Comtrex; Contac Cold and Flu; Coricidin; Dimetapp Cold and Fever; Drixoral Cold and Flu; Excedrin; Multi-Symptom Formula Midol; Panadol; Robitussin Cold, Cough, and Flu; Sinarest; Sine-Aid; Sine-Off; Sinutab; Sudafed Cold; Sudafed Sinus; TheraFlu; Tylenol; Vicks NyQuil)	There is no apparent link to birth defects, but there is a possible association with fetal renal failure.
Aluminum hydroxide (found in antacids such as Gaviscon, Maalox, Mylanta)	There is no apparent link to birth defects, but some studies have indicated that excessive use may be associated with neonatal calcium or magnesium imbalance.
Aspirin (acetylsalicylic acid) (found in aspirin compounds such as Alka-Seltzer, Bayer, Bufferin)	There is no apparent link to birth defects, although there is some conflicting data on that front. Can cause clotting disorders with possible fetal and maternal hemorrhage when taken in large doses close to term. Other possible effects are low birthweight, prolonged gestation and labor, and neonatal cardiac problems. Low-dose aspirin use is recommended, however, for treatment of certain causes of repeated miscarriage or autoimmune disorders such as lupus.

Medications Guide

Active Ingredient	Possible Problems During Pregnancy
Attapulgite (found in antidiarrheals such as Donnagel and Kaopectate)	There are no available reports of use during pregnancy.
Bacitracin Zinc (found in antibiotic ointments such as Mycitracin, Neosporin, Polysporin)	There is no apparent link to birth defects.
Benzocaine (found in topical anesthetics such as Americaine, Cepacol, Hurricaine, Chloraseptic)	There are no available reports of use during pregnancy.
Bisacodyl (found in laxatives such as Correctol, Dulcolax)	There are no available reports of use during pregnancy.
Bismuth Subsalicylate (found in products for upset stomach, indigestion, and so on, such as Pepto-Bismol)	Should be used only during the first five months of pregnancy and in amounts that do not exceed the recommended dosages.
Brompheniramine Maleate (found in antihistamines such as Dimetapp, Vicks DayQuil)	There is a possible association with birth defects. What's more, use of antihistamines in last two weeks of pregnancy increases the risk of a neonatal eye problem known as retrolental fibroplasia. Note: If you need an antihistamine, your doctor is most likely to recommend Benadryl.
Caffeine (found in certain analgesics, including Excedrin)	There is no apparent link to birth defects, although some studies have indicated that high doses may be associated with miscarriage and infertility.
Calcium Carbonate (found in antacids such as Tums)	No adverse effects have been proven with usual dosages.
Camphor (found in anti-itch and local anesthetic products and nasal inhalers such as Afrin, Mentholatum, Vicks VapoRub)	No adverse effects have been proven from topical use.

Medications Guide

Active Ingredient	Possible Problems During Pregnancy
Chlorpheniramine Maleate (found in antihistamines such as Alka-Seltzer Plus, Chlor-Trimeton Allergy, Comtrex Maximum Strength, Contac, Coricidin, PediaCare, Sinarest, Sine-Off, Sinutab, TheraFlu, Triaminic, Tylenol Allergy)	There is no apparent link to birth defects. See *Brompheniramine Maleate*.
Clotrimazole (found in antifungal/yeast infection products such as Canesten)	There is no apparent link to birth defects.
Dexbrompheniramine (found in antihistamines such as Drixoral)	There is no apparent link to birth defects. See *Brompheniramine Maleate*.
Dextromethorphan (found in cough suppressants such as Alka-Seltzer Plus Cold and Cough, Comtrex, Contac Cold, Dimetapp Cold, Robitussin, Sudafed Cold and Cough, Triaminic, Tylenol Cold, Vicks 44)	There is a possible link to birth defects. Use as directed by your physician and avoid using preparations containing alcohol wherever possible. (Note: If your doctor recommends that you use a cough syrup that contains alcohol, try not to panic. The amount of alcohol contained in a teaspoonful or two of cough syrup is not sufficiently high to raise serious concerns about fetal alcohol syndrome.)
Dimenhydrinate (found in anti-nausea products such as Gravol)	Generally considered to be safe for use during pregnancy.
Diphenhydramine (found in antihistamines such as Actifed, Benadryl, Contac, Sine-Off Night Time, Tylenol Allergy, Tylenol PM)	This active ingredient may be responsible for cleft palate and other birth defects, but research to date has been inconclusive.
Docusate (found in certain types of laxatives)	Chronic use may cause a fetal magnesium imbalance.

Medications Guide

Active Ingredient	Possible Problems During Pregnancy
Doxylamine (used as a sleep aid in products such as Alka Seltzer Plus Night-Time Cold, Robitussin Night-Time Cold, Unisom Nighttime, and Vicks NyQuil)	This active ingredient may be responsible for skeletal, limb, and cardiac defects; cleft palate; and gastrointestinal malformations. Research to date has been inconclusive.
Ephedrine (used in decongestants such as Primatene Tablets)	This active ingredient may be responsible for heart-rate disturbances, minor birth defects, hernias, and club-foot, but research to date has been inconclusive.
Guaifenesin (found in expectorants such as Benylin, Novahistine, Primatene Tablets, Robitussin, Sudafed Cold, Vicks 44E)	There is no apparent link to birth defects.
Hydrocortisone (topical) (used in topical and hemorrhoid sprays and ointments such as Anusol HC-1 Hydrocortisone, Cortaid, Cortizone, Nupercainal Hydrocortisone, Preparation H Hydrocortisone 1%)	There are no available reports of use during pregnancy. Anusol HC-1 and 1% topical hydrocortisone are widely prescribed for use during pregnancy.
Ibuprofen (used in aspirin substitutes such as Advil, Motrin IB, Nuprin)	There is no apparent link to birth defects, but third-trimester use can cause fetal cardiac malfunction.
Magnesium Carbonate/Magnesium Hydroxide/ Magnesium Trisilacate (used in antacids such as Ascriptin, Bufferin, Di-Gel, Gaviscon, Maalox, Mylanta, Phillips Milk of Magnesia, Rolaids, Vanquish)	There are no adverse effects proven with usual dosages, but chronic or excessive use may be associated with neonatal calcium or magnesium imbalance.
Meclizine (used in antinausea products such as Bonamine, Dramamine)	This active ingredient causes birth defects in some animals, but there is no apparent link to birth defects in humans.

Medications Guide

Active Ingredient	Possible Problems During Pregnancy
Menthol (used in cough and sore throat preparations and in soothing ointments such as Afrin, BenGay, Cepacol, Eucalyptamint, Gold Bond, Hall's Cough Drops, Listerine, Mentholatum, Vicks Chloraseptic, Vicks Cough Drops)	There are no available reports of use during pregnancy.
Miconazole (used in products that treat yeast/fungal infections, such as Lotrimin, Monistat)	There is no apparent link to birth defects.
Oxymetazoline (used in nasal decongestant sprays such as Afrin, Neo-Synephrine, Vicks Sinex)	There is no apparent link to birth defects, but excessive use could impair uterine blood flow.
Phenolphthalein (used in laxatives such as Dialose, Ex-Lax, Phillips Gelcaps)	There is no apparent link to birth defects.
Phenylephrine (used in nasal decongestant sprays and hemorrhoid creams such as Afrin, 4-Way Fast Acting Nasal Spray, Hemorid, Neo-Synephrine, Preparation H, Vicks Sinex)	This active ingredient causes birth defects in animals. May be responsible for minor birth defects: hernia and clubfoot. (These studies do not apply to topical creams.) Excessive use could impair uterine blood flow.
Phenylpropanolamine (used in decongestants and appetite suppressants such as Acutrim, Comtrex, Contac, Dexatrim, Dimetapp, Robitussin-CF, Tavist-D, Triaminic, Vicks DayQuil Allergy)	This active ingredient may cause eye and ear defects and other anomalies, but the research is inconclusive. Excessive use could impair uterine blood flow.

Medications Guide

Active Ingredient	Possible Problems During Pregnancy
Pseudoephedrine (used in decongestants such as Actifed, Advil Cold and Sinus, Alka-Seltzer Plus, Allerest, Benadryl Allergy/Cold, Comtrex, Contac, Dimetapp, Robitussin Cold, Sine-Off, Sinutab, Sudafed, TheraFlu, Triaminic, Tylenol Allergy, Tylenol Cold, Vicks 44D, Vicks DayQuil, Vicks NyQuil)	This active ingredient may be responsible for heart rate disturbances, minor birth defects, hernias, and clubfoot, but research is inconclusive.
Psyllium (a natural fiber that promotes normal bowel movements, used in laxatives such as Metamucil)	There are no available reports of use during pregnancy. Because it's not absorbed into the bloodstream, it's considered safe for use.
Pyrethrins with piperonyl butoxide (used in anti-lice lotions and shampoos such as A-200, EndLice, Pronto, R & C, Rid)	This is the preferred drug for treating lice infestations during pregnancy.
Simethicone (used in anti-flatulents such as Di-Gel, Gas-X, Maalox, Mylanta, 3M Titralac, Tums)	There is a possible association with cardiovascular birth defects, but cause and effect is not likely.
Sodium Bicarbonate (used in antacids such as Alka-Seltzer, Arm & Hammer Pure Baking Soda)	There are no adverse effects proven with usual dosages.
Sodium Chloride (table salt), used in nasal sprays such as Afrin, Ocean Nasal Mist	Considered safe for use during pregnancy.

Adapted from a similar chart in The Unofficial Guide to Having A Baby *by Ann Douglas and John R. Sussman, M.D. (Wiley Publishing, 1999).*

When to Seek Help

When to Call Your Caregiver During Pregnancy

As a rule, you should call your caregiver immediately if you experience one or more of the following symptoms:

- **Heavy vaginal bleeding or clotting, or the passage of tissue from the vagina:** You may be experiencing a miscarriage. If this happens later in pregnancy (during the second or third trimesters), you may be experiencing placenta previa or a placental abruption.

- **Lighter vaginal bleeding that lasts for more than one day, or is accompanied by pain, fever, or chills:** You may be experiencing a miscarriage. If this happens later in pregnancy (that is, during the second or third trimesters), you may be experiencing placenta previa or a placental abruption. If there's bleeding behind the placenta, you could be developing chorioamnionitis (an infection of the membranes surrounding the fetus).

- **Severe abdominal or shoulder pain that may be accompanied by spotting or bleeding or the passage of tissue:** Your pregnancy may be ectopic (the embryo may have implanted somewhere other than in the uterus) and you may be experiencing internal bleeding as a result. This typically occurs at six to eight weeks of pregnancy, but can also occur when your pregnancy is a little further along.

- **A severe or persistent headache (particularly one accompanied by dizziness, faintness, or blurry vision):** You may be developing high blood pressure or preeclampsia (a serious medical condition characterized by high blood pressure).

- **Dehydration (dry mouth, thirst, reduced urine output, low-grade fever):** You may be becoming dehydrated, which puts you at risk of experiencing premature labor.

When to Seek Help

- **A fever of more than 101°F:** You may have an infection that requires treatment. Even if you don't, your caregiver will want to bring your temperature down because an elevated core body temperature can be harmful to the developing baby and may trigger premature labor.

- **Painful urination:** You may have developed a urinary tract infection, which can trigger premature labor and/or lead to a kidney infection.

- **A watery discharge from the vagina:** Your membranes may have ruptured.

- **Sudden swelling of the face, hands, or feet:** You may be developing preeclampsia.

- **The symptoms of premature labor (uterine contractions, vaginal bleeding or discharge, vaginal pressure or pressure in the pelvic area, menstrual-like cramping, a dull backache, stomach or intestinal cramping and gas pains, a general feeling of unwellness):** You may be experiencing premature labor (see page 241).

- **A significant decrease in fetal movement after the 24th week of pregnancy:** Your baby may be experiencing problems in the womb.

When to Seek Help

When to Call Your Caregiver After Delivery

You need to get in touch with your caregiver immediately if you experience one or more of the following symptoms, which may indicate that you are experiencing a postpartum hemorrhage, a postpartum infection, or other postpartum complications:

- Sudden, heavy bleeding

- A large number of blood clots

- The return of bright red bleeding after your lochia (postpartum bleeding/discharge) has begun to subside

- Foul-smelling vaginal discharge

- Severe pain or redness around, or discharge from, an episiotomy, tear, or cesarean-section incision

- Fever over 100°F

- Nausea or vomiting

- Pain, redness, hot spots, red streaks on breasts

- Painful, burning urination

- Painful, swollen, or tender legs

- Persistent perineal pain with increased tenderness

- Vaginal pain that worsens or lasts longer than a couple of weeks

- Severe pain in your lower abdomen

Symptoms of Premature Labor

If you find yourself experiencing one or more of the following symptoms, you could be experiencing premature labor, and you should get in touch with your doctor or midwife immediately.

- **Uterine contractions (tightening) that may or may not be painful:** While it's normal to experience some uterine tightening when you're exercising, you should be concerned if these contractions continue after you stop exercising; if they don't go away when you drink a large glass of water or juice, empty your bladder, and lie down on your side; and if you continue to have more than four contractions over the course of an hour.

- **Vaginal bleeding or a change in the quantity or quality of your vaginal discharge:** Look for discharge that's brown- or pinkish-tinged and more mucusy or watery than normal.

- **Vaginal pressure, or pressure in the pelvic area:** You may experience a feeling of pressure in the pelvic area or the vagina that radiates toward your thighs, or you may feel as though the baby is falling out.

- **Menstrual-like cramping in the lower abdomen:** If you experience menstrual-like cramping in your lower abdomen — either continuous or intermittent — you may be going into labor.

- **A dull backache:** If a dull backache radiates to the side or the front of your body and isn't alleviated by any change in position, you could be going into labor.

- **Stomach or intestinal cramping and gas pains:** If you experience cramping, gas pains, diarrhea, nausea, or feelings of indigestion, you could be going into labor.

- **A general feeling of unwellness:** Don't underestimate your gut feeling. If you feel unwell and your body is telling you that something's wrong, it's possible that you're going into labor.

Emergency Childbirth Procedures

Delivering Your Baby If You're Alone

Getting help

1. **Try to remain calm.**

2. **Call the emergency-response number in your community** and ask the person who takes the call to send out an emergency-response team and to notify your doctor or midwife that you're about to deliver your baby.

3. **Ask a friend or neighbor to stay with you** until the emergency-response team arrives. (If you're able to find someone, they should follow the tips below on helping a mother who's about to give birth.)

Preparing for the birth

1. **Wash your hands and your vulvar area** with mild detergent or soap and water.

2. **Spread a shower curtain, a plastic tablecloth, clean towels, newspapers, or sheets on a bed, sofa, or the floor,** and then lie down until someone arrives to assist you.

Coping during labor

1. **If you feel the urge to push, try panting, instead.** It will help you to hold off on pushing until someone arrives to help deliver your baby.

2. **If your baby starts coming before help arrives, gently ease the baby out of your body** by pushing each time you feel the urge and catching the baby with your hands.

After the birth

1. **Lay the baby across your abdomen or put the baby to your breast** if the umbilical cord is long enough to reach.

2. **Don't try to pull the placenta out.** If the placenta is delivered before help arrives, wrap it in towels or a newspaper and keep it elevated above the level of the baby.

3. **Do not try to cut the cord on your own.** Wait until help arrives.

Emergency Childbirth Procedures

Assisting a Woman Who's About to Give Birth

What to do first

1. **Remain calm.** Instead of panicking, focus your energies on comforting and reassuring the mother.

2. **Call the emergency-response number in your community** and ask the person who takes the call to send out an emergency-response team and to notify the mother's doctor or midwife that she's about to deliver her baby.

Preparing for the delivery

1. **Wash your hands and the mother's vulvar area** with mild detergent or soap and water.

2. **Spread a shower curtain, a plastic tablecloth, clean towels, newspapers, or sheets on a bed or table.**

3. **Help the mother sit at the edge of the bed or table with her buttocks hanging off and her knees apart.** Support her head with one or two pillows.

4. **If she's in active labor and in too much pain to climb onto the bed or table, place a stack of newspapers or folded towels under her buttocks** so that she'll be far enough off the floor for you to be able to deliver the baby's shoulders easily.

5. **If you're in a vehicle, help the mother lie down on the seat.** Then help her to position herself so that she has one foot on the floor and the other on the seat.

Assisting the mother during labor

1. If the mother needs to vomit, help her turn her head to the side so that her mouth and airway will remain clear.

2. Use a dishpan or basin to catch the amniotic fluid and blood.

3. Encourage the mother to start panting if she feels the urge to push. This may help to delay the birth until help arrives.

Delivering the baby

1. Once the baby's heard starts to crown (to emerge through the tissues at the opening of the vagina), encourage the mother to pant or blow. This will help to slow the baby's exit from the birth canal. Then, to keep the baby's head from emerging too quickly, you should apply gentle counterpressure to the baby's head.

2. If you see a loop of umbilical cord around the baby's neck, gently pull on it and lift it over the baby's head.

3. If the baby's amniotic sac is intact when the baby's head emerges, puncture the sac with a clean fingernail or a ballpoint pen, being sure to hold the pen away from the baby's face, and carefully move the sac away from the baby's mouth.

4. Take the baby's head in your hands and press it slightly downward, asking the mother to push at the same time. Then help to ease the baby's shoulders out one at a time. Once the baby's shoulders have been delivered, the rest of the baby should slip out easily.

5. Clear the baby's mouth and nose immediately after the birth, using a bulb syringe and gauze pad (if you have them) or by gently stroking the sides of the baby's nose in a downward direction, and the neck and underside of the chin in an upward direction to help expel mucus and amniotic fluid. You can also try holding the baby's head lower than its body to use gravity to drain away the fluid. Once the baby starts crying vigorously, you can return the baby to an upright position.

After the birth

1. **Wrap the baby in a clean blanket or towel and lay the baby across the mother's abdomen or place it at her breast** if the cord is long enough.

2. **Don't try to pull the placenta out.** If the placenta is delivered before help arrives, wrap it in towels or a newspaper and keep it elevated above the level of the baby.

3. **Do not try to cut the cord before help arrives.**

4. **Keep the mother comfortable and the baby warm and dry until help arrives.**

Postpartum Depression

As wonderful as motherhood can be, it's not unusual to be hit with the "baby blues" — that hormone-driven wave of emotion that tends to come crashing over you one to three days after the birth. You may be at risk of experiencing a more serious form of baby blues — postpartum depression — if you can check off any of the following:

- You have a family history of postpartum depression

- You've experienced major depressive episodes in the past

- You have a history of hormonal problems (such as PMS)

- You experienced fertility problems prior to conceiving and/or repeated pregnancy losses, something that can cause your expectations of parenthood to be sky-high, leading to almost inevitable disappointment

- You just delivered your first baby prematurely or by cesarean section

- You just delivered multiples

- You had a very short or very long gap between pregnancies

- You left the hospital within 24 hours of the birth

- You're experiencing a lot of financial stress

- You and your partner are having relationship problems

- You're not used to spending a lot of time at home (for example, you've just quit your full-time job and are at home for the very first time)

- You're alone a lot or otherwise lack family support

- You experienced the death of a parent during childhood or adolescence

Postpartum Depression

You may be suffering from postpartum depression if you experience one or more of the following symptoms on an ongoing basis. If you suspect you're experiencing postpartum depression, seek help from your caregiver.

- Difficulty making decisions
- Feelings of inadequacy (for example, feeling incapable of caring for your baby)
- A fear of being left alone
- A fear of an impending disaster
- Feeling like you don't want the baby
- A powerful desire to run away
- Panic attacks and/or extreme anxiety
- Feeling like your life is out of control
- A lack of interest in activities you've always enjoyed
- Insomnia and/or nightmares
- Eating disturbances
- Feeling helpless or suicidal

Fortunately, the prognosis for women who develop postpartum depression is good: Approximately 95% of women will experience an improvement within three months of starting treatment, and 65% will recover within a year. The key is to identify the problem early on: Studies have indicated that health-care professionals frequently fail to pick up the signs of postpartum depression in new mothers and, consequently, many women struggle unnecessarily with this highly debilitating disorder.

Nutrition on the Go for Busy Moms

These foods have been chosen because they take just seconds to prepare and they can be enjoyed with a baby in your arms. Best of all, they work equally well at mealtime and snack time and are all highly versatile.

- Yogurt mixed with cereal and diced fruit
- Fruit-and-yogurt shakes
- Hard-boiled eggs
- Low-fat cheese
- Sliced meat
- Hummus and other spreads/dips
- English muffins, bagels, or pitas
- Bran muffins
- Whole grain crackers
- Dried fruits and nuts
- Fresh fruits
- Fresh vegetable, such as baby carrots
- Salads in bags (stuff the salad in a pita to make it easier to eat when you're holding a baby)

Your Calendar Pages

The following pages give you month-long calendars for you to customize and use during the next ten months of your life.

Use these pages to keep track of your prenatal checkups, dental and eye appointments, baby showers and other get-togethers, prenatal classes, time out with your girlfriends, romantic evenings with your partner (they may not happen too often after your baby is born!), a pre-baby vacation before your seventh month, and work-related meetings and deadlines.

By keeping all your tasks and appointments in one place, you don't have to juggle more than one calendar or planner during your pregnancy — and you'll never miss an important deadline or appointment.

Month _____

Monday	Tuesday	Wednesday	Thursday	Friday	Saturday	Sunday

Month _____

Monday	Tuesday	Wednesday	Thursday	Friday	Saturday	Sunday

Month _____

Monday	Tuesday	Wednesday	Thursday	Friday	Saturday	Sunday

Month _____

Monday	Tuesday	Wednesday	Thursday	Friday	Saturday	Sunday

Month _____

Monday	Tuesday	Wednesday	Thursday	Friday	Saturday	Sunday

Month _____

Monday	Tuesday	Wednesday	Thursday	Friday	Saturday	Sunday

Month _____

Monday	Tuesday	Wednesday	Thursday	Friday	Saturday	Sunday

Month _____

Monday	Tuesday	Wednesday	Thursday	Friday	Saturday	Sunday

Month _____

Monday	Tuesday	Wednesday	Thursday	Friday	Saturday	Sunday

Month _____

Monday	Tuesday	Wednesday	Thursday	Friday	Saturday	Sunday

Check Out These Other titles from The Mother of All Parenting Authors!

—m—

Whether you're looking for advice on sailing through nine months of pregnancy, coping with the terrible twos, or instilling confidence and independence in your pre-teen, Ann Douglas is by your side, offering comforting, medically sound, and non-bossy information for every stage of parenting. Don't miss any of these great resources:

The Mother of All Pregnancy Books: Whether you're thinking of starting a family, overjoyed (and a little nervous!) that the test came back positive, or well into your pregnancy, Ann Douglas is right there with you. Covering everything including nutrition, medications, your baby's development, and what you'll experience during the birth, this calm, reassuring book will step you through this exciting time.

The Mother of All Baby Books: The instruction manual that Mother Nature forgot to include with your new bundle of joy, this book is the only reference you'll need for your baby's first year. Jam-packed with medically sound information, this must-have guide gives you the skinny on everything from nutrition and development to sleeping patterns, breastfeeding, and immunization. No new parent should be without it!

The Mother of All Toddler Books: What parent hasn't heard of – and dreaded – the terrible twos? In this insightful and often humorous book, Ann Douglas explains what goes on in the toddler's mind, and why they behave the way they do. This resource is chockful of invaluable information including how to get started potty training, when to move your toddler from a crib to a bed, how to initiate engaging activities with your child, and what types of discipline are appropriate for this age group. Ann Douglas will help you not only survive this developmentally rich time, but also enjoy it.

The Mother of All Parenting Books: Ann Douglas helps you put it all together in this witty and perceptive book, providing practical tips and fantastic advice on such timely topics as helping your kids build a healthy lifestyle and body image; avoiding parent burnout; keeping your kids safe without smothering them; and creating harmony between siblings.

Don't miss any of these great titles, available wherever you buy books.